ARLEN ROTH'S
COMPLETE
ACOUSTIC GUITAR

ARLEN ROTH'S COMPLETE ACOUSTIC GUITAR

ARLEN ROTH

SCHIRMER BOOKS
An Imprint of Simon & Schuster Macmillan
NEW YORK

Prentice Hall International
LONDON · MEXICO CITY · NEW DELHI · SINGAPORE · SYDNEY · TORONTO

Schirmer Books
An Imprint of Simon & Schuster Macmillan
1633 Broadway, New York, NY 10019-6785

Library of Congress Catalog Card Number: 85-22286

Printed in the United States of America

printing number
        6   7   8   9   10

All instructional photos by Deborah Roth.

Library of Congress Cataloging-in-Publication Data

Roth, Arlen.
    Arlen Roth's Complete acoustic guitar.

    Includes index.
    1. Guitar—Instruction and study. I. Title.
II. Title: Complete acoustic guitar.
MT580.R66 1985   787.6'1'0712   85-22286
ISBN 0-02-872150-0

For Gillian and Deborah, my best buddies

CONTENTS

ACKNOWLEDGMENTS

There are several people who deserve special thanks for their important contributions to this book, and to my ability to create it.

I first want to thank Terry Nakamoto, the great designer and craftsman at Yamaha who built the masterpiece guitar for me that is used in the majority of this book's photos. I also want to thank Atsushi Muramatsu, Joe Ieki, John Nuerenberg, and Chuck Thompson at Yamaha; and Marc Dronge at Guild Guitars for their invaluable help. I must thank all of the artists with whom I've worked, particularly Paul Simon and Art Garfunkel, for helping me reach a better understanding of the art of acoustic guitar playing. I thank everyone at *Guitar Player* magazine, particularly Tom Wheeler, Jim Crockett, Don Menn, and Dan Forte. My thanks go also to Phil Hood and Jim Hatlo of *Frets* magazine, as well as Jon Sievert for his photographic assistance. For their terrific help with my manuscript, I wish to thank Joe Dalton and my wife, Deborah. The inimitable George Gruhn deserves a load of thanks for his photos of some great guitars, and I want to give a special tip of the hat to Stan Jay and Hap Kuffner—The Mandolin Brothers. For their able assistance and patience, I must thank my editor, Maribeth Payne, and my agent Arthur Schwartz. Most of all, thank you Merle, Chet, Son, Bukka, Tampa, Robert, Doc, Clarence, Leadbelly, Phil and Don, John and Paul, Elvis, and others too numerous to name, for being my deepest inspiration.

INTRODUCTION

Guitar has certainly come a long way from the days when it was considered primarily an instrument for vocal accompaniment. The acoustic, non-amplified guitar is of course the oldest, and thereby has the longest story to tell. One really can't expect this entire tale to unfold in the pages of a single book, yet our time spent together learning is an important chapter in the acoustic guitar's ongoing evolution. When I say The *Complete* Acoustic Guitar, I am referring to the steel-string acoustic guitar, with all of its past taken naturally into the process. This, after all, is what music is—that ongoing, never-ending process by which this lovely language is constantly redefined by its interpreters. That is why for one to become a *complete* acoustic guitarist, as in many art forms, he or she must become aware of what has come before, and what is taking place right now. I should point out that this book will deal *only* with the steel-string acoustic guitar and *not* the classical guitar, a study that in and of itself could take up volumes.

During the course of my development as a player, I was obsessed with a desire to understand the richness of history represented by this instrument in my arms. This desire came naturally to me, because I was fortunate enough to grow up in a household where the arts and their *roots* were deeply encouraged. When interested in country music, I didn't seek out the latest John Denver record. Rather, I would scour the pawn shops and old record stores for rare Jimmie Rodgers or Hank Williams records. For a rural kid in Appalachia this may not seem so difficult, or even interesting, for that matter. But for a kid from the streets of the Bronx, it was a major revelation! The same goes for my discovery of the blues. I certainly wasn't going to let The Blues Project or Cream become my guiding light, although these groups did help to introduce the blues to an audience that would have otherwise turned a deaf ear. Upon getting the initial spark from these bands of the mid and late 1960s, particularly the Paul Butterfield Blues Band with Mike Bloomfield on guitar, I actively pursued the artists to whom these artists listened. In other words, I developed a habit of going to the source. Urged onward by friends and fellow musicians, I hunted down recordings by Robert Johnson, Son House, Bukka White, Blind Blake, Willie McTell, and just about any other early blues artist I could find. This period helped develop my taste for slide, or bottleneck guitar; I will cover this unique and important style in the pages that follow.

Besides bottleneck, you'll find sections on blues, country flatpick, and fingerpicking styles; ragtime guitar; open tunings; and lead, rock, and jazz guitar. I've also set aside a chapter for a discussion of the guitars themselves in hopes of helping readers make a better decision in choosing instruments. As an added bonus, I felt that no learning experience should go without some advice from a teacher with hard-earned skills. Therefore, I wrote a chapter that draws from my 15 years as a professional studio and touring guitarist. During this time I acquired quite a bit of knowledge that can be passed along. These years of experience are certainly the greatest music school of all, and I feel it is important to share some of what I learned from being at such a unique vantage point.

From sleeping on the floor of vans while travelling cross-country, to touring as lead guitarist with Simon and Garfunkel in what was one of the largest shows ever to tour, you can see that I've covered a lot of useful terrain, and that it can be of use to you, the student.

Above all, we must not lose sight of the fact that guitar is mainly a means of expression. Of course, the technical aspects are of great importance, and we shall not ignore them in this book. But it's *where* all this technique is leading you that is really the heart of the matter. Developing your own style, finding your own sound—these are what musicians strive for. I merely wish to give you the tools and the advice with which you can go forth and develop your own sound. Guitar, particularly the acoustic steel-string variety, takes a lot of hard work and dedication. Ideally, this hard work should be undertaken as a form of pleasure. I rarely recall a time when I considered my playing to be "practice." Because I was self-taught, there was no one looking over my shoulder telling me what and when to play. Rather, it was my own desire and joy that drove me onward to play and create, developing my own goals in the process. Over the course of this book, I hope this story starts to unfold for you as well, and that by the time you're done, you'll be ready to go on and do your own creating, perhaps referring back to the book now and then for just a *touch* of inspiration!

ARLEN ROTH'S COMPLETE ACOUSTIC GUITAR

1

THE FUNDAMENTALS OF ACOUSTIC GUITAR PLAYING

I assume that even before you picked up this book, you had a working knowledge of the guitar and how it is played. However, in case you've already acquired some bad habits of which you might not be aware, let us go over some of the true fundamentals of acoustic guitar playing so we can get started on the right foot.

HOLDING THE GUITAR

Sitting is perhaps the most usual and comfortable way of playing the acoustic guitar. In many performing circumstances I still opt for the sitting position, even though standing would add to the show-like quality of the performance. In the classical position (first photo), we see that the guitar is placed on the left leg, with the foot elevated by a footrest. This position is generally associated with classical and flamenco playing, neither of which are covered in this book. However, from time to time you may feel the urge to play in this manner, and you'll find it a very comfortable position for the steel-string acoustic guitar.

In the standard position (second photo), we see that the guitar is on the other leg, and is held much more horizontally. This position is well-suited to flatpicking as well as fingerpicking, and I would advise its use in most cases.

Seated—Classical Position

Seated—Standard Position

Standing, providing of course that your guitar can accommodate a guitar strap, is really my second choice for acoustic guitar playing (see photo). It's fine for strumming, but for intricate single-note work I find that the guitar can tend to "get away" from me when I'm playing. For electric guitars, standing is fine, but acoustics tend to be too bulky or wide to be handled in a subtle way. In any event, here is the position I recommend most if you intend to stand with the guitar. Note that the neck is angled upward so that the left hand need not be involved in supporting the instrument, only with fretting the notes properly.

THE PICK

Guitar picks come in a seemingly endless array of shapes, sizes, thicknesses, and materials these days. The photo illustrates a choice of some of the more common and not so common types you might come across. I prefer perhaps the most popular pick of all—the semi-

Proper Standing Position.

triangular pick with two rounded ends in a *medium* thickness. This pick is neither so big as to be cumbersome, nor so small that it will get lost, and the medium thickness enables me to handle both gentle and aggressive passages with equal control.

A unique collection of picks.

As far as holding the pick is concerned, the following photograph illustrates the proper position. The pick should not be held too firmly or loosely. By holding it at the end, with only a small amount exposed, we don't even have to consider using a tight grip, because so little of the pick is actually being used.

Holding the pick.

SETTING UP THE GUITAR

Steel strings are not easy to play. When first trying to do so, you may react in a way just short of being traumatized. This is of course due to the fact that your fingers haven't become accustomed to the sharp metal strings, and haven't developed proper calluses to deal with the problem. Now, with all of this going against you in the beginning, you certainly don't want to compound the problem by having a guitar that is physically handicapping! The way a guitar should feel to you is largely a matter of personal preference. However, when you're just starting out, there are some rules to follow. Later on, when you've made a more complete adjustment to your instrument, you'll know what subtle changes should be made to accommodate *your* touch.

ACTION

Your guitar's "action," or string height and tension, is crucial to playing comfort. Some acoustic guitars have adjustable bridges, while a great many do not, and must have their stationary bridges filed down by a guitar craftsman, or luthier. I've always been a firm believer in having the action just high enough so there is some real effort behind the notes. This will provide a much cleaner, clearer tone, eliminating the buzzing that might occur as a result of having the strings set too low. If the strings are too high, it will become apparent to you after playing for some time, because things just won't be getting any easier!

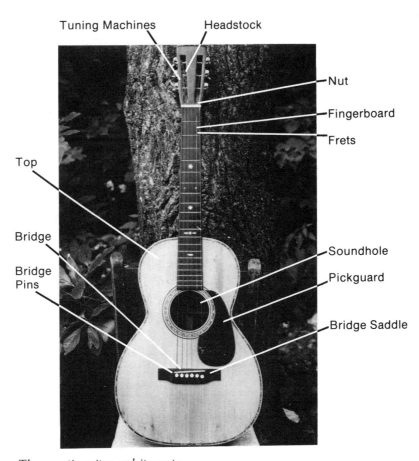

Tuning Machines · Headstock · Nut · Fingerboard · Frets · Top · Bridge · Bridge Pins · Soundhole · Pickguard · Bridge Saddle

The acoustic guitar and its parts.

If they're *really* too high, you'll actually experience noticeable intonation problems when pressing the strings down. Another consideration is to have the guitar set up just high enough for slide playing, and just low enough for fretting. I do this because I often like to double on both techniques on the same instrument.

When troubleshooting your action problems, make sure to check the nut to see if in fact the strings are set too deeply or not deeply enough. You should also make sure that the top is not lifting from being pulled by the bridge, or that the bridge itself isn't pulling off

Note the height of the strings over the fretboard.

the top of the guitar. These two situations are serious, and besides causing action problems, they can render serious, permanent damage to the instrument if not tended to by a qualified luthier as soon as possible. Neck warpage or bowing is also a major problem, but as most guitars now have adjustable truss rods running through the neck, it's a problem that, in the right hands, can be quickly remedied. This photograph shows the string height at the twelfth fret of my most often-used guitar.

STRINGS

What strings you use on your guitar is also a matter of personal preference, and the choice really depends on what you want to get out of the instrument. Currently in the United States there are actually only five or six major string manufacturers, and these companies, while having their own brand names, also make hundreds of other brands for different companies. These strings are basically the same, yet you still can't convince many guitarists who absolutely *swear* by their particular, sometimes obscure, favorite!

As for the material the strings are made of, there are primarily two acoustic types made from alloys on the market: bronze-wound and phosphor bronze-wound. You'll find that the phosphor bronze strings are slightly warmer in sound, and they last a fair amount longer than the bronze or brass variety. Personally, I prefer the less popular bronze-wound because of its more sensitive sound. You should be your own judge, however, and try out the different types before you decide.

With regard to string gauge, this again depends on your own sound and technique, what you want out of the guitar, and how the instrument is constructed. These days, most new acoustic guitars are built to handle medium-gauge strings, and usually come factory-equipped with them. These are fine for strumming or fingerpicking, but the guitar would have to be extremely "soft," (bend easily) or have a very short scale (the length from nut to bridge) if you expect to do any serious stringbending. Strings of this diameter are also unadvisable if you expect to retune the guitar to any of the higher open tunings. I prefer and recommend standard light-gauge strings for most applications, and find that the combination of the light string with the medium pick is just right. If your guitar has had medium- or heavy-gauge strings on it for a long time, you might find that the neck requires some minor adjustments after changing to the lighter gauge. If you want to maintain mediums on the guitar, you should make sure, through the services of a reputable repairman, that your guitar is constructed heavily enough to withstand the string tension. Problems such as the bridge lifting up, the top pulling up, or the neck warping or twisting could arise. Please be careful about this particular point.

READING TABLATURE, SYMBOLS, AND STANDARD NOTATION

Learning to read music well is, for some, a lifelong venture. It takes an incredible amount of practice and discipline, and is often not achieved by many musicians. Because the guitar is an instrument that is so easily "picked up" by ear, its players are perhaps the least likely of all musicians to read music. This is not to say that reading music isn't important, however, for it can open doors to new pieces of music that you'd never dreamed of attempting to play! The study necessary to make you a truly great reader would easily require a whole other book, so for the most part, we'll stick to the basics. First, here are the notes, and how they appear on the fingerboard.

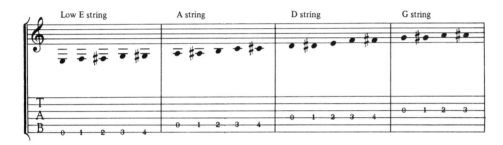

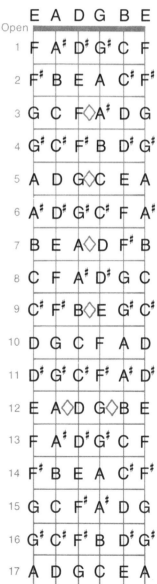

Rhythmic Notation

How long or short we play a note is called its *time value*, and is, of course, essential to the phrasing of musical passages. In this book, and in much of western music, the measures are played in four/quarter, or 4/4 time. This simply means that there are four beats to the measure, and that each is of a one-quarter note time value. Here, we see the measure with four even quarter notes.

A half note is called so because it consists of two quarter-notes, dividing the 4/4 measure in half.

A whole note has no stem, and its time value consists of all four quarter-notes.

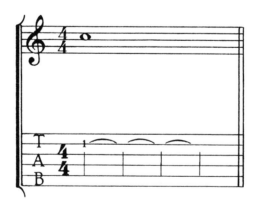

Measures can also be broken up into eighth notes, each getting half the value of a quarter note.

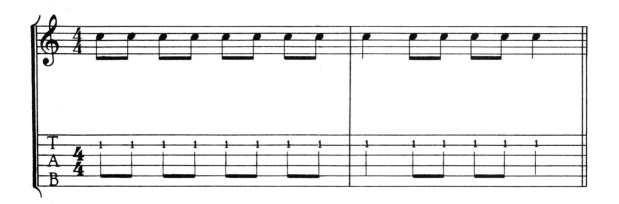

When we play triplets, we are dividing up the 4/4 measure into four groups of 3, or 12 notes all together. This type of rhythmic figure is sometimes written as 12/8 time, and there is usually a 3 with an arch over each group of triplets.

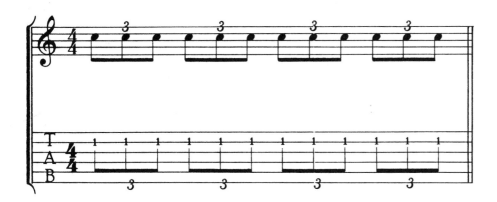

This type of even division is fairly endless, and there are sixteenth, thirty-second, and even sixty-fourth notes.

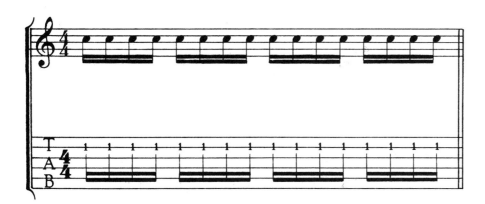

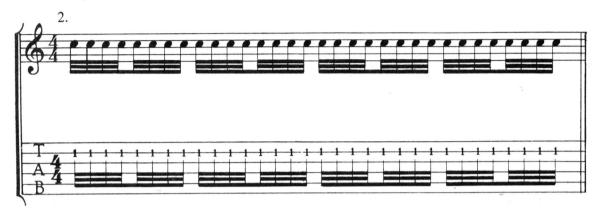

A dotted note receives an extra half of its time value. This is how we would represent a note that receives three quarter-notes worth of time value.

Here we see how the "triplet" feel can be created with dotted eighth notes. This is the well-known shuffle approach to blues and jazz playing.

We can also indicate a note's time extension by the use of *ties*. When the note is tied to an additional note of the same pitch, it receives that additional time value. To see some of the various possibilities, study the next diagram carefully.

Rests indicate periods where we don't play; they also have time values. Here is how they're written for the various durations, and how they'll appear in the tablature as well.

In this diagram, we see how the various rhythmic values of both the notes and the rests can be put together. As a practice, try *tapping* out the rhythms with your hand while maintaining the four/quarter (4/4) beat in your head. Try to keep it going, even if you make a mistake.

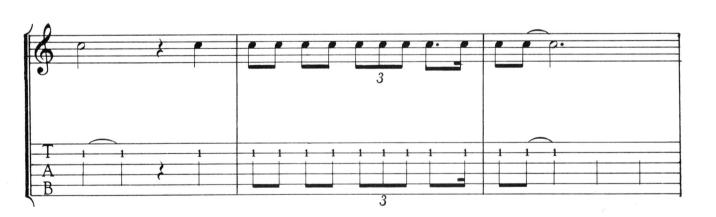

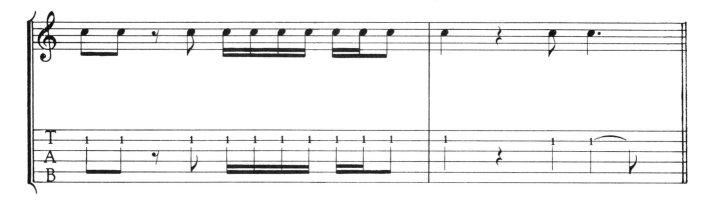

Reading Tablature and Symbols

For those of you who cannot read music, and for those who can and would like an additional aid, I've provided guitar tablature below all of the standard notation in this book. Tablature consists simply of six horizontal lines, representing the six strings of the guitar, with the high E string at the top.

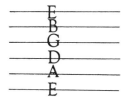

Any number you'll see intersecting a line (string) represents the number fret at which we depress that given string. For example, this is how we would represent a C chord in tablature form.

Symbols

Throughout the book, I will call upon special symbols to represent certain guitar techniques. These will appear in both the tablature and standard notation.

An arch between two notes with an "s" over it indicates that you slide between those notes.

If that same arch has an "h" over it, this indicates a **hammer-on** between those two notes. In this case, the first note is played with the pick, while the second is created solely with the finger that is "hammering-on" and fretting it higher up on the fingerboard.

If the arch has a "p" over it, this means that there is a *pull-off* between the notes. In this case, the second note is sounded by a downward "pluck" off of the first note. This technique often immediately follows a hammer-on.

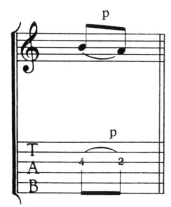

When the arch has a "b" over it, this indicates a *bend*. In bending a note you can raise its pitch by staying on the same fret, and then pushing or pulling the string in either direction. In this case, the first note is bent, thereby making it sound like the second note. Hence, the use of parentheses around the second note.

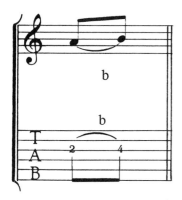

An "r" indicates a *release* of a bend, usually following a bend, as in this example.

There are times when the release occurs alone. In this case, the note was already bent up to pitch *before* the release occurred.

A straight line pointing up or down *toward* a note means you slide *to* that note from a point approximately two or three frets below or above it. This same line pointing *away* from the note indicates a slide after the note is sounded.

If the note is to be played with *vibrato*, it will have a wavy line over it. We'll discuss proper vibrato technique later on in the book.

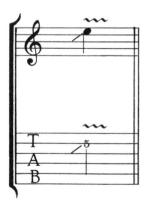

CHECKLIST OF CHORDS

In Diagram 1 is a group of chords you should have as a basic part of your guitar knowledge. It should also act as a guide to refer back to from time to time should you feel uncertain about a given chord's position or fingering.

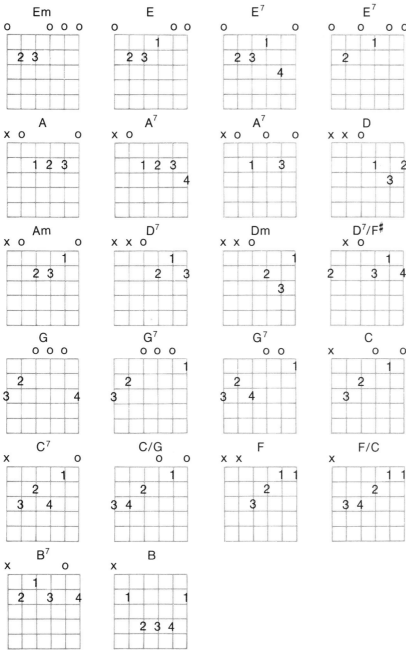

Diagram 1. Chord Checklist

2

ACOUSTIC FLATPICKING: COUNTRY/FOLK STYLES

RHYTHM GUITAR

Rhythm guitar can fall into many categories. There is, of course, the use of the guitar as a rhythm instrument that accompanies a voice in a solo situation. This is probably the most common practice on the part of most guitarists, but there is a much greater role the rhythm guitarist can play, and this art form gets more complex every year. With the advent of the guitar boom and the increase in group music, the rhythm guitarist has been an increasingly important contributor to the sound of this music. In the days of the big bands, the guitar, usually an arch-top variety, was limited as strictly a rhythmic "comping" instrument. It was so hard to distinguish among all the loud brass that one could only hope for the coarse brushing of the strings to cut through the sound. Often, there would be only one guitarist in these orchestras, and prior to Charlie Christian's amplified work with Benny Goodman, no big-band musician played single-note guitar. However, in the more contained forms of group playing such as country, rural blues, folk, and bluegrass, the rhythm guitar often had to weave itself with other lead *string* instruments, more often than not, another guitar. This helped set up the "two-guitar" sound that has grown into a widely diversified practice, and has won rhythm guitar playing greater respect as a true art form.

In acoustic music, which is the variety discussed in this book, rhythm guitar relies even more on use of the right hand than does the more sustaining electric guitar. In the case of bluegrass bands, for example, the guitar is traditionally played in a very hard-driving manner, with an occasional bass note run thrown in as a "fill." We'll start developing our right-hand technique in the section that follows on bluegrass rhythms.

Bluegrass Rhythms—Strums and Fills

In learning this style of playing, you'll be developing a picking technique that employs the subtle use of an alternation between bass notes and chord work. This requires a supple wrist action, and you should apply the same rules of holding the pick as I stated in Chapter 1.

In this initial exercise, we are playing the "basic country strum" in the key of G. Each time we play a chord here, it's divided between a bass note that acts as a downbeat, and an "answer" of the chord being strummed twice: once down away from you, and once in a very natural upstroke that returns to the original position. The pattern is always: *down, down-up, down, down-up*, etc. Here it is for the key of G, with each chord getting a full measure's worth of time.

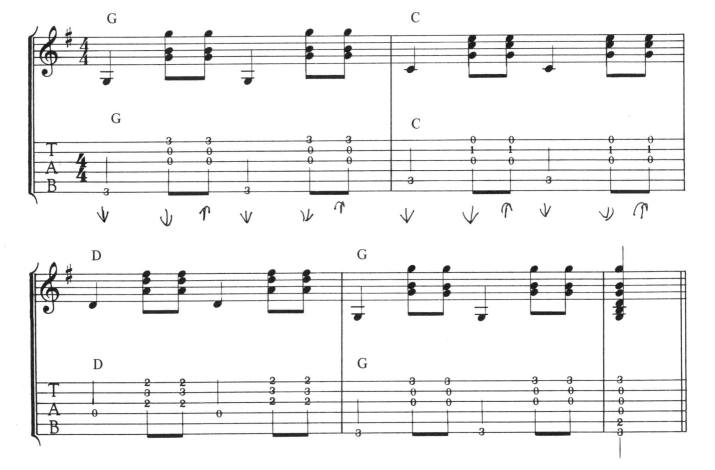

In this next piece, we see how we can now play connecting "lead-up" runs between chords. This gives a greater feeling of movement to the music, while developing skill in single-note playing. Make sure to play all of the single-note runs with downstrokes.

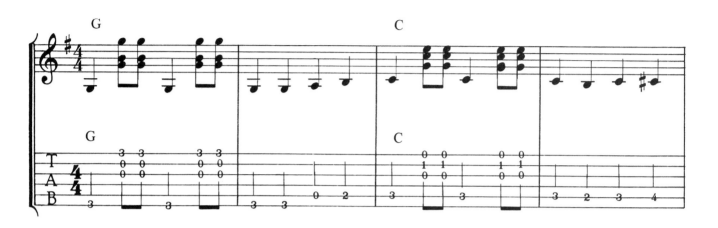

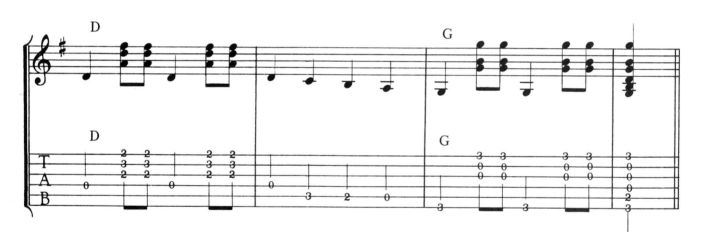

In the next exercise, we will, for the first time, utilize *alternating* bass notes as part of our rhythm lick. As a result, we have a country exercise that consists of all the previous techniques: bass notes, lead-ups, strums, *and* alternating bass notes. Please note that these alternations require great accuracy with the pick. This does not mean that you should grip the pick more tightly, as many people mistakenly do. Rather, you should maintain the same relaxed approach as before, relying upon the wrist for accuracy. You'll also notice that the C chord requires an alternating bass note that is *below* the original C bass, requiring the third finger actually to alternate between the third fret on the A string and the third fret on the low E string. All these alternated notes should still be exclusively played with downstrokes.

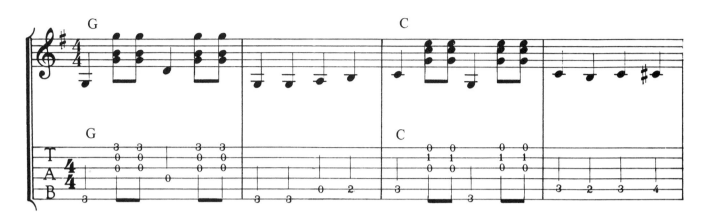

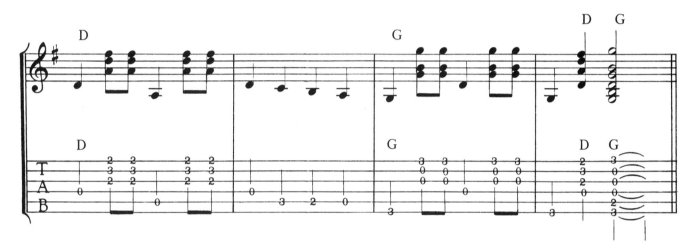

Hammer-Ons

Hammer-ons are one of the most useful tools a guitarist can acquire for his or her repertoire. With this technique, we can now create one or more additional notes after the first note is picked, without picking the string a second time. Of course, we are now getting more involved in left-hand technique, and you'll be amazed at the feeling of accomplishment and versatility that the wonderful technique of hammering-on can bring.

In this exercise, we'll be using the hammer-on licks as a substitute for one of the previous alternated bass notes. The open string is picked on the beat, and the second finger comes down and hammers the note at the second fret, resolving and completing the chord. You should make sure to start the hammer-on from as low a point above the fretboard as possible with as much controlled strength as you can. This will greatly increase your accuracy, and will develop proper hammer-on technique.

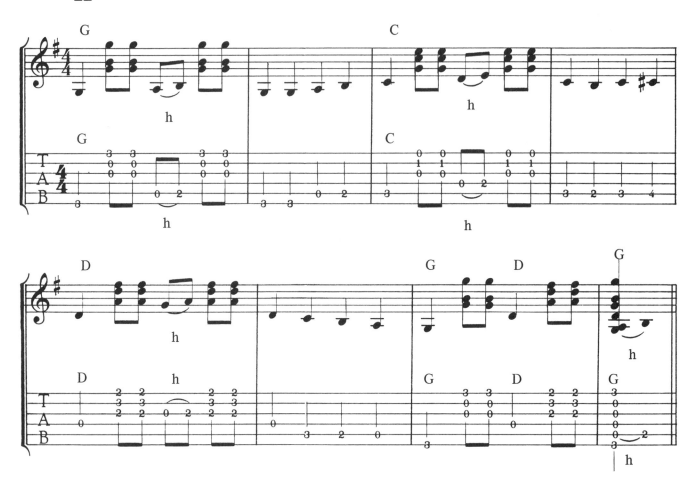

In the case of most country-style hammer-ons, the note we are hammering *to* is the major third of that particular chord. This is almost invariably from a whole step (two frets) below it, and is an integral part of the country sound. In the following group of chord exercises, we see the positions for this major third hammer-on in all of the familiar open positions. Note that in the case of E and B7 we are forced to make the hammer-on a half step in distance, due to the particular nature of these chord positions.

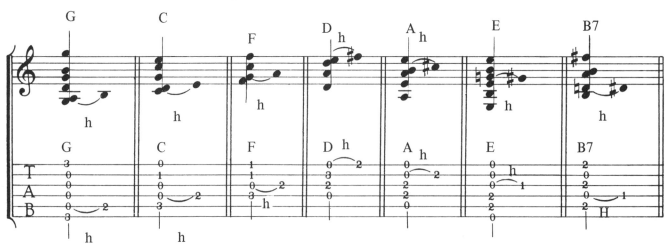

More Complex Hammer-Ons

The technique of using a hammer-on within a chord can be extended so that the hammering finger does more "roaming," creating additional hammer-ons on other available strings. This gives more of a lead guitarlike quality to the rhythm lick, and certainly is a more complex usage of hammer-on technique. In this exercise we see how within both the G and C chords we can use the same finger on the same fret on two different strings to create this kind of movement.

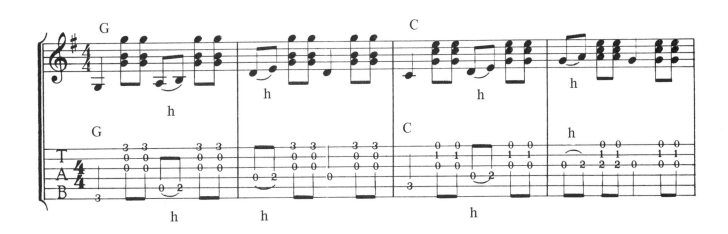

Synchronized Melody and Rhythm Pattern: "Wildwood Flower"

One very useful application of this technique is the ability to play a synchronized melody along with the rhythm pattern that is being maintained. This is a wonderful technique and deserves a great deal of attention if you intend to become a total flatpicker. In the song that follows, the country classic "Wildwood Flower," we see this technique put to great use. The melody runs smoothly through the rhythm pattern, enabling the rhythm strums to act as a kind of "fill" between the lead lines. It may take a while before this song sounds right to you, so please don't give up. Any guitar technique that involves the synchronizing of two or more parts presents as many rewards as hardships, so it's surely worth the effort!

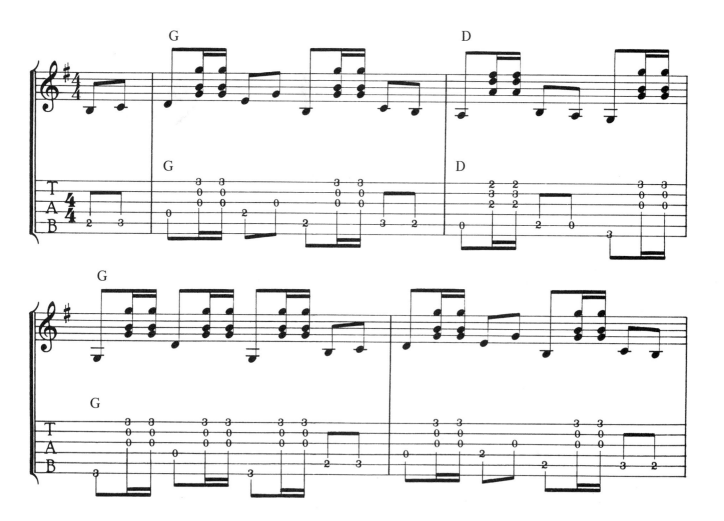

The Bluegrass Run

In traditional bluegrass music, there is rarely any soloistic work by the guitarist. Aside from the single-note work we've been incorporating into rhythm patterns, there is one run or lick that has shown up repeatedly in all forms of country guitar playing. I like to call this lick the "bluegrass run" because it is most often heard as an intro or an ending, played by the guitar, in acoustic bluegrass music. Of course it has found its way into the mainstream as a result of its undeniably catchy, recognizable quality, and therefore deserves a lot of attention.

I've written the bluegrass run in several keys so that you can take note of the fundamental differences and similarities between these positions. Also, for the first time, you should play these with an alternated up–down picking motion. Note that the first part of the lick uses a two-note hammer-on, something that we're also seeing for the first time. This consists of one downstroke, then two notes following each other that are hammered consecutively.

Here we have a country melody and rhythm combination piece that shows where this bluegrass lick can best be used, both as a melody and as a fill.

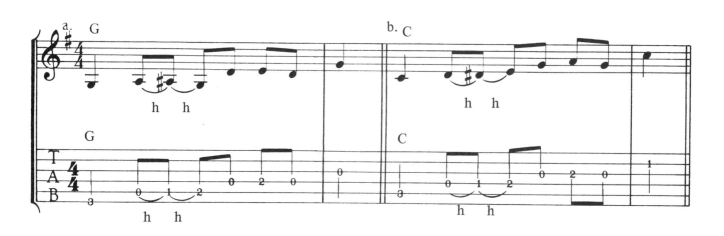

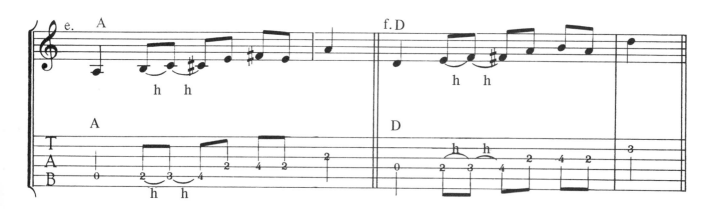

LEAD GUITAR

A lead guitarist assumes many responsibilities. For one, he or she must be sensitive to the melody of the song, which requires a trained ear and considerable experience. Often, as a lead player, you'll be called upon to solo or fill, and this improvisational ability is the heart and soul of lead playing. Of course, there must be a development of tone, attack, phrasing, and technique that goes along with the ear-training skills one must have to become a lead guitarist. These are some of the issues we will deal with in this section. The problem of being able to make musical statements with a solo is paramount, and the notes you play must convey to the listener and your fellow musicians that you are aware of what is going on harmonically and rhythmically. This, of course, takes much experience, yet there are some fundamental stumbling blocks I can help you get over.

The Major Pentatonic Scales

In playing country lead guitar, no scale receives so much attention as does the major pentatonic. It consists of five notes, hence the "pentatonic" label, and generally helps to create a rather optimistic, "up" musical feeling. The pentatonic scale is basically the major scale with a few notes omitted. For example, Diagram 2 shows the open position of the major scale for the key of G, followed by the major *pentatonic* scale in the same position.

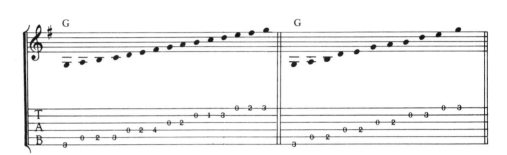

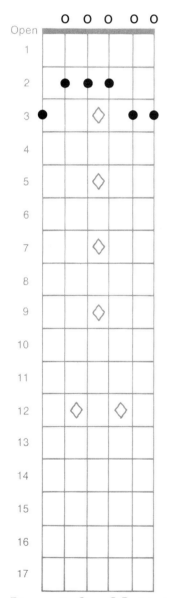

As a practice, you should run through this scale, in an up-and-down motion, as written in the exercise that follows. Try to play it with even up-and-down picking strokes.

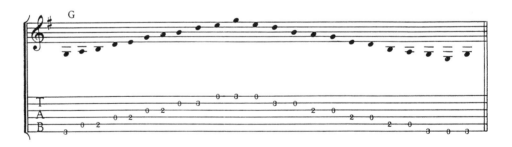

As a good example of how hammer-ons can be incorporated into this scale, I've supplied the following exercise. In this run, we pick only the open strings, then hammer-on the note for each string. Please remember to keep those hammers coming from as short a distance above the strings as possible.

Diagram 2. Open G Pentatonic Scale

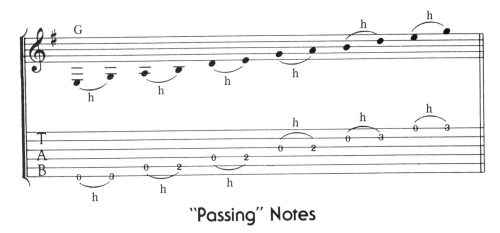

"Passing" Notes

This and all the other scales are sources for improvisation and creation. In fact, if you study the bluegrass run we learned earlier, you'll notice its source is the pentatonic scale we just worked on, with one fundamental difference: we are now adding "passing" notes within the position. This particular label comes from the fact that the added note actually serves to "pass" from one note of the scale to another by moving in half steps. In both the bluegrass lick and the scale that follows, the one note that creates the difference is the minor or flatted third of the scale. Here we see a common occurrence within country and blues idioms, that of using a "blue" or dissonant note that is *not* part of the major scale. This clash in tonality creates the "blue" note sound, and works well in quick "passing" status because of its rather discordant sound.

Here we see how and where these notes can be incorporated into the open major pentatonic scale. Take care in switching from the flatted third on the G string to the major third of the open B.

The *flatted fifth* of the scale is also a marvelous "passing" tone and offers countless possibilities for improvisation and creativity. Here we see it incorporated into the scale by adding the fourth (C) and then using the flat five (C sharp [♯]) as part of a chromatic run from the fourth to the fifth. As in the case of the flatted third, it has two positions within this particular pattern.

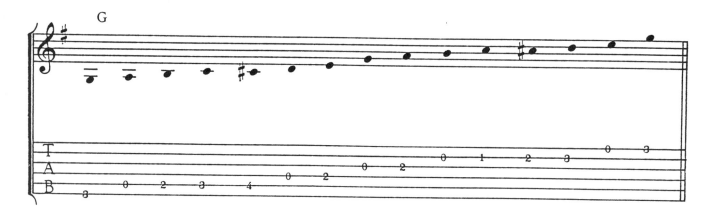

Licks and Exercises

The following group of licks and exercises is designed to show some of the many possibilities that can arise with this scale and the flatted fifths and thirds at your disposal. I have kept the phrasing rather simple for now, as this is our first attempt at playing real acoustic lead guitar licks.

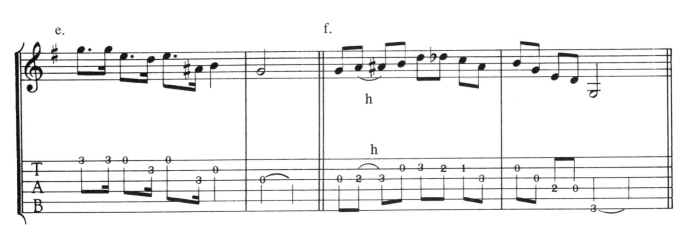

Diagram 3's position of the pentatonic scale is really a physical extension of Diagram 2's. All we are now doing is adding a new, higher position at the end of the scale, adding more notes, and increasing our creative potential. Note that between the second and the fourth frets on the G string, we are now utilizing a *slide*. This technique enables us to shift positions completely while keeping the same finger on the string, and is an invaluable tool for the lead guitarist. Note also that at the end of the scale we have an additional, higher octave of the same slide.

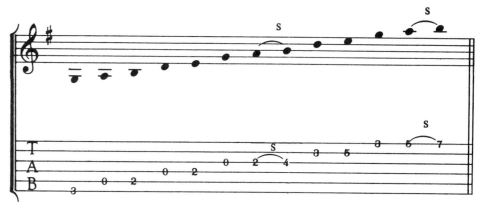

In this example we see how the flatted third passing notes fit into this more extended pentatonic position. The notes are in the same places, only now we fret the B note at the fourth fret of the G string rather than playing the open B.

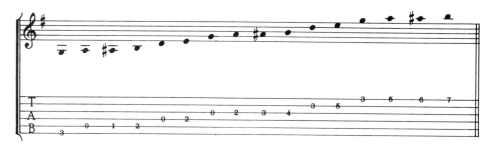

The flatted fifths also work well with this form of the pentatonic scale, and here we discover another position at the sixth fret of the G string. This position, I might add, is a source for a *wealth* of blues runs.

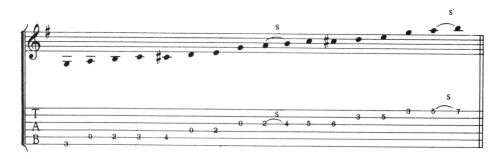

The following is a group of runs developed from this particular position. Note how many of them combine the lower "open" form with the "closed" higher notes. Make sure to use the "slides" where indicated, because they will greatly add to the unique character of the lick.

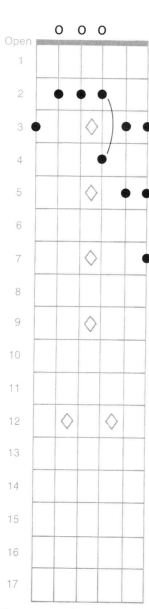

Diagram 3. G Pentatonic Scale #2

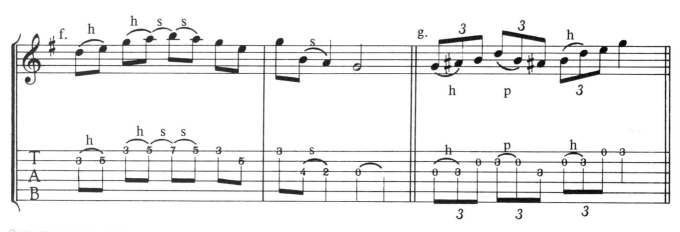

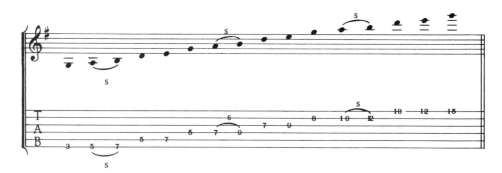

In Diagram 4 we see an example of the longest variety of pentatonic scales, this time for the key of G. This may well be one of the longest scales, in distance, on the guitar. Again, play it with the slides I've indicated so you can see just where and how this scale shifts positions.

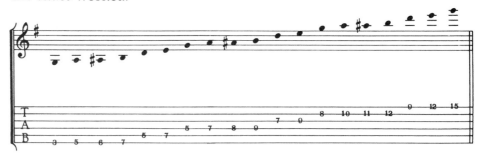

The flatted third passing notes are best fretted by the same finger that played the note just below them. In this way we maintain the movement required to keep the positions shifting in the same way that the slides worked.

The flatted fifths are harder to reach within this scale because of its more extended positions. Therefore, we must stretch the left hand more in order to reach these passing tones. This requires a more direct, "straight-over" hand position that relates strongly to the playing of classical guitarists.

Diagram 4. G Pentatonic Scale #3

Here are a special group of licks to learn from this very extended pentatonic scale. At times we'll use a chromatic fingering style for the flat fives and thirds, while at other times we'll use one- or two-fret slides for a similar effect.

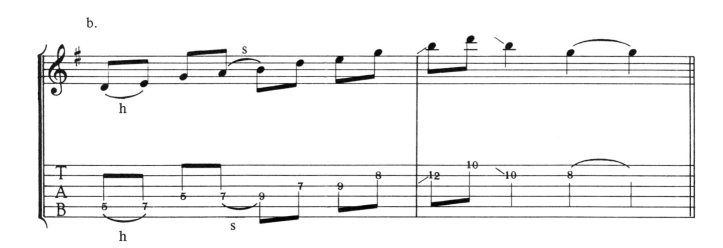

Incorporating the Techniques

These exercises, actually extended solos, truly combine and bring to life all of the elements we've been discussing. The lead guitarist is at a great advantage by having these many expressive tools at his or her disposal. In addition, the lead player simply gets more of an opportunity to use these techniques than the rhythm player, and therefore masters them more easily. Hammer-ons, pull-offs, and slides are the three techniques that we'll be using in the following country-style solo pieces. Take special care in the phrasing of these exercises, because subtlety is what separates the great from the not-so-great players, and fostering it is the main purpose in my writing these exercises for you.

This first piece, in the key of G, incorporates the three techniques into the first and second positions of the pentatonic scale. Notice that even though the chords change, your position remains relatively stationary, and "works around" the new chord change within the original scale.

This exercise, written with the longest pentatonic position in mind, really shows just how much of the neck you can cover with a scale this extensive. You'll see how sliding can create major position shifts within a very short span of time, and can help in developing your speed and accuracy.

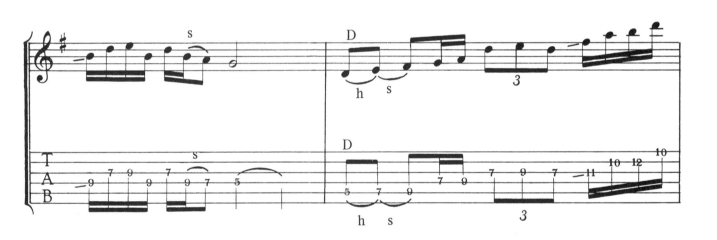

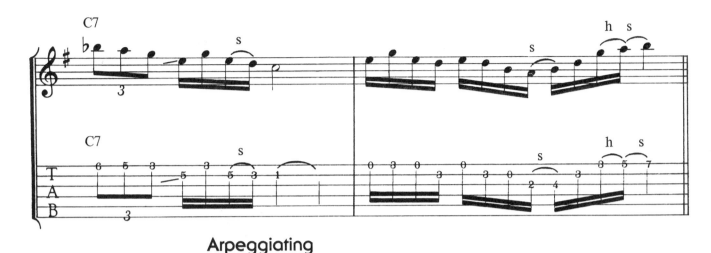

Arpeggiating

Now that we've begun to see how scales can actually work within chord changes, we should make a point of learning perhaps the most frequently used form of chordal lead work; arpeggiating. An arpeggio is really nothing more than the notes of a chord, played one at a time to create a melody. This relieves much of the work load for the left hand, because it can hold down the chord's position while the picking hand does the single-note work. Here, for example, is a simple arpeggio exercise that illustrates how we could break up six-string barre chord positions.

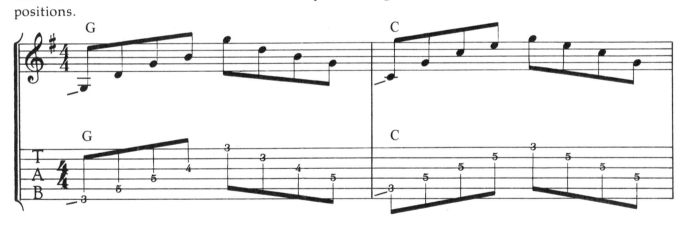

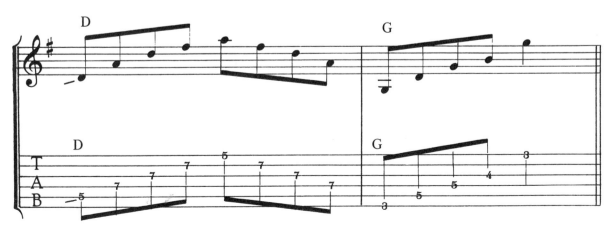

Now, for the same chords, we'll play it more like a lead guitarist, arpeggiating "partial" forms of the chords. Remember to fret only the required notes.

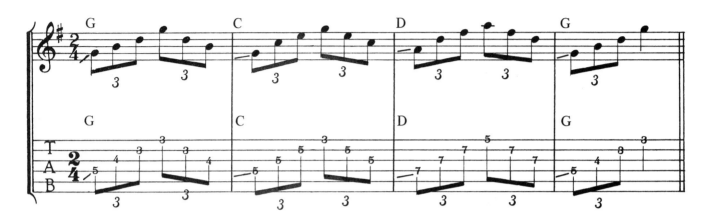

The partial C form is very important and often used for both arpeggios and chordal work, and, combined with the A form barre, can make for some very fluid, easily shifting positions. Here we see two photos, one of the A barre form, and then the partial C form as it looks placed right on top of it.

Second fret A chord barre.

Partial C form of D on top of an A chord.

This exercise is one of my personal favorites, because if you really execute the arpeggios properly, the feeling is one of strong musicality. Try playing it first with all downstrokes; then, when you can pick up the tempo, try alternating strokes: *down–up–down.*

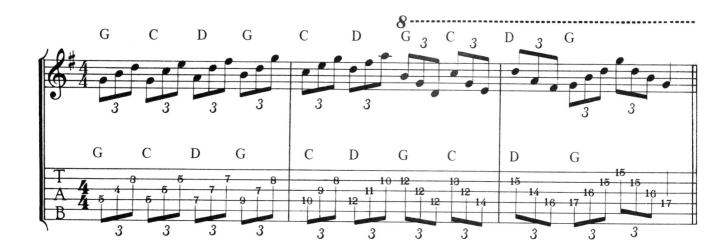

This piece, using another of my favorite sounds, places the partial C form over the A-form barre with the use of hammer-ons. This is a particularly beautiful sounding style, and as you can see, there are essentially two ways of using these hammer-ons: individually played notes, hammered one at a time, or all the notes hammered at once.

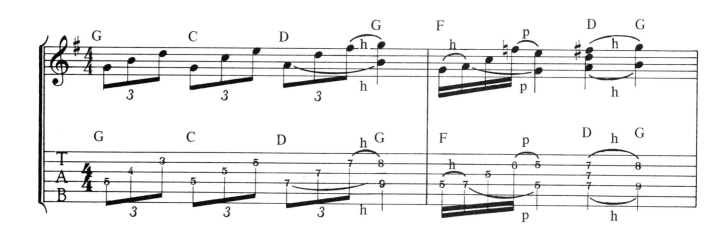

This piece adds one more important element to this particular style: that of "pulling-off" the C-form chord as well as hammering-on. Remember that the pull-off is really a left-hand "pluck" downward, giving new life to the string's vibration.

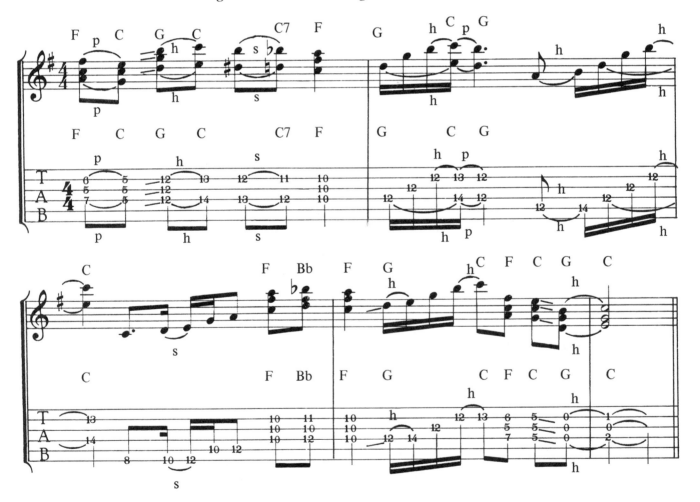

Chromatic Style Playing

When you're talking about truly developing the right hand's speed and accuracy, chromatic style picking is the best way to go. Now that we've been concentrating upon the fretting hand for quite awhile, you should feel at home enough on the fingerboard to begin work on this rather difficult right-hand technique.

To first illustrate exactly what I mean by chromatic picking, here is an open position chromatic scale exercise. Be sure to use up-and-down strokes with the pick, while trying to make the notes sound even in both volume and sustain.

Now, moved up to a *closed* position, with no open strings being played, we see how it becomes a bit more difficult to execute the left-hand stretches that are required. To help facilitate this stretching, try to assume a more "straight over" left-hand angle as many classical and jazz players do.

This photo illustrates the proper left-hand position, and depicts the pinky on the fourth chromatic note of the low E string (G♯). Note the angle of the hand, and how it's arched over the fretboard to obtain the

Left-hand position during the fourth note of the chromatic scale.

best possible results. This position requires the thumb to be well behind the neck, running right down the middle, acting as a center of gravity for the rest of the hand.

As far as the scales we've covered are concerned, there is an endless series of places where chromatic runs can be found with relative ease. One rule I follow that would be good for you to apply in your search for new licks is, wherever you find groups of scale notes separated by whole steps with similar related positions on adjacent strings, you can experiment with chromatic runs.

In the exercise that follows, I've taken the long pentatonic scale in G and turned it into a continuous flow of three-note, three-fingered chromatic runs. Not all of these notes must always be used, but it's a good way to see just how many places they can exist. As a good practice, I've indicated in both the music and the tablature exactly where you shift positions and begin your three-note pattern all over again with the index finger. The goal is to get the index finger in the right

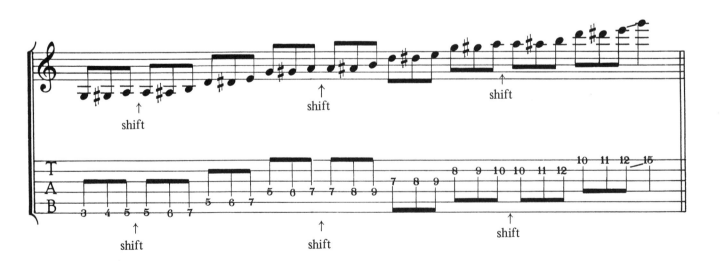

location just in time to allow the picking to remain smooth and consistent. Try it slowly at first, building up speed as you become more acquainted with the positions for both hands.

In these two treble-string exercises we see two of the most often-tapped areas for single-string chromatic country work. Ideally, these positions should start with the B-string run played by the second, third, and fourth fingers. The switch, then, to the high E string is played by the first, second, and third fingers, respectively. I for one, however, have found that I can "cheat" just a little by using only the first three fingers for these runs on any string, but remember, your picking must be *fast* and *clean* to take a chance like that!

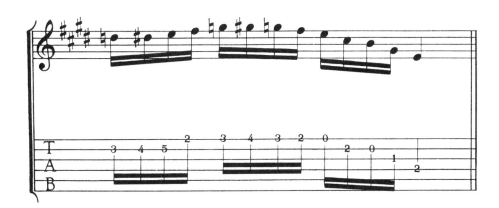

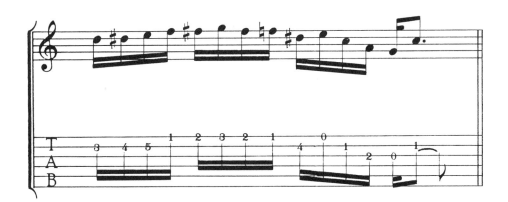

Chromatic Pentatonic Licks

This group of licks illustrates just some of the countless positions and approaches that can be found within the chromatic style. Please take time to find some new ones on your own; I know you'll be successful, and the feeling of accomplishment will be just fantastic. This, after all, is the most I could ever wish for when you read my book: that you learn to create your own style from the ideas I give you.

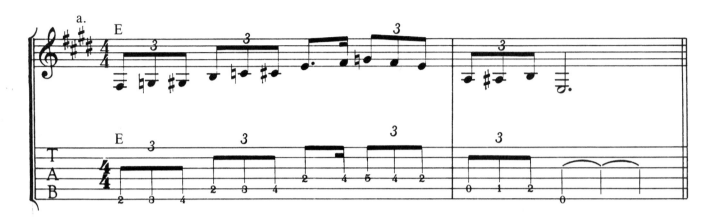

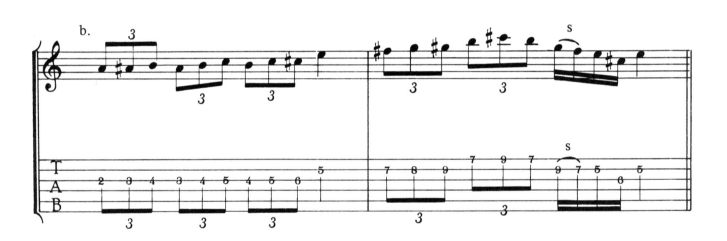

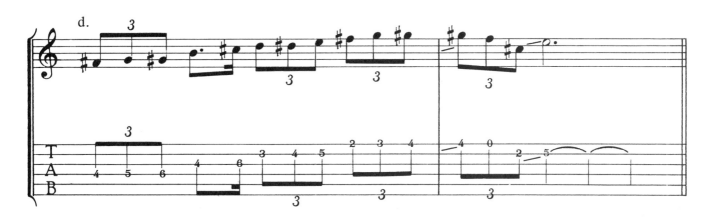

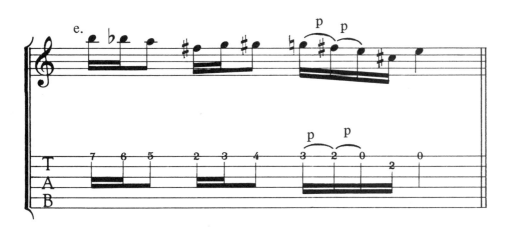

The Technique of Doc Watson

No study of acoustic country guitar styles, particularly in the chromatic flatpicking vein, would be complete without Doc Watson, the genius of rapid-fire picking. Doc's influence has spread far and wide, and we can attribute an entirely new style and a whole generation of pickers to his inspiration. He was the first rural acoustic player to truly "amaze" urban audiences in the early 1960s with his dazzling, fast technique, and he has continued to be a driving, creative force on the acoustic music scene.

One thing to keep in mind about Doc's picking style is that he uses the rather unorthodox up-and-down forearm movement, with a relatively stiff wrist position. This, for most, is an extremely difficult way in which to play, although it does increase volume and attack. I still believe in using a nice, relaxed wrist for this kind of picking technique, however, and I also feel that this can bring about the broadest range of subtleties with the pick. The following photo illustrates what I feel is the proper position for rapid-fire picking with a relaxed wrist.

Keep your wrist relaxed.

Doc Watson.

"Black Mountain Rag"

In the following piece, one of Doc Watson's greatest classics, you see how chromatic-style picking plays a part in becoming the melody of a song that is then improvised upon. Keep in mind that the pick should strike each string at the same angle, necessitating movement of the arm and wrist up or down to whatever string is required to maintain the proper angle, as in the photo.

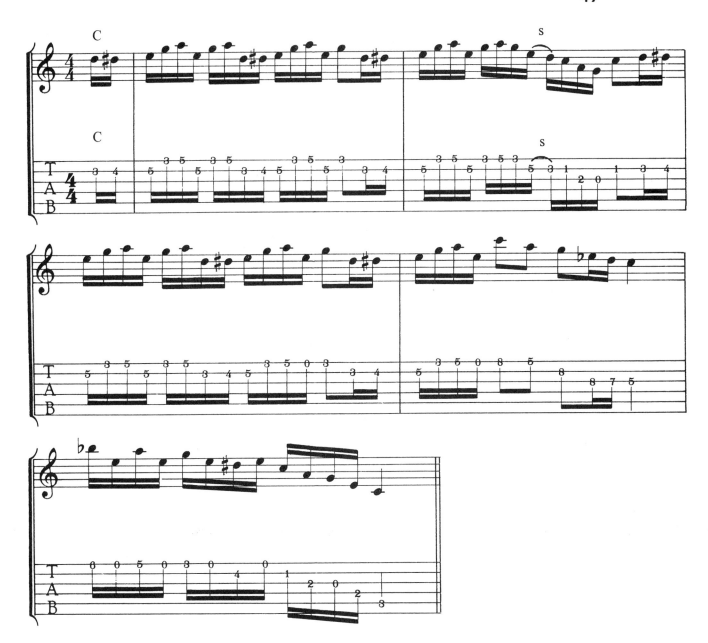

STRING BENDING

String bending has always been one of my favorite guitar-related subjects due to the fact that it has been extremely successful for me over the years. My style was mostly evolved on the electric guitar, an obvious choice because the electric guitar's strings are much thinner and easier to bend than an acoustic's. This, however, did not deter me from developing a string-bending style on the acoustic, even though the strings were quite a bit heavier, and the possibilities were somewhat limited. I've seen players who put light-gauge electric strings on

The late Clarence White, one of the finest acoustic and electric guitarists the world has ever known. (Photo courtesy of Gene Parsons)

acoustic guitars to help their string bending, particularly benefiting from the unwound G, or third string. This, however, is usually on the acoustic/electric variety of guitar, with pickups to help the volume and sustain. If you were to attempt this on a regular acoustic guitar, you'd be able to bend the strings more easily, but you'd be severely sacrificing the instrument's sound and projection. I prefer to stay with a normal set of acoustic guitar strings, including a wound G, and to be limited on *that* string only as far as bending distance is concerned.

By "bending" the string, we are raising its pitch to a note that is determined by the control of the finger that is actually doing the bend. This requires great control, and on the acoustic guitar in particular, requires many hours, days, even *years* of practice.

The Act of String Bending

This "control" of the bent note I just mentioned is the real secret behind great string-bending technique. I'm sure I'm not the first teacher who has seen first-time students boast of their 15 or so years of playing, only to find they had no idea of how to properly bend a string!

As far as the actual act of bending is concerned, being able to bend the note *cleanly* is a major objective. Playing cleanly on the guitar basically means that when the note is sounded, there should be no other extraneous notes, or, more to the point, *sounds* that accidentally occur. Good right-hand technique is essential here, but in the case of string bending, which is *such* a demanding left-hand technique, we must be extra careful with our left hand as well as our right. One of the really important rules to follow is: always use whatever other fingers are available *below* the actual bending finger to help the bend along. This serves a dual purpose as it should also help to "push" the other strings out of the way for the particular string that is bent. When releasing the bend, as is often the follow-up, these fingers, by staying on those same strings, serve to "damp" out any overtones or errant notes that might occur.

Here is a very descriptive photo that illustrates just how this position should look. In this case, I'm bending the B string up a whole step (two frets) with my third finger, and using the first and second fingers to help bend and push.

The photo illustrates a bend going *toward* the guitar player. In the case of the lower strings, a bend *away* from the player would probably

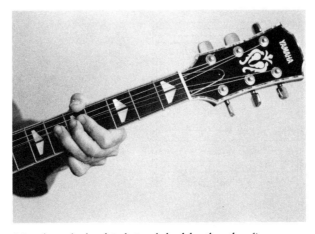

Note how the bend is being helped by the other fingers.

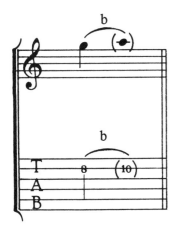

be more advisable. Note that in both cases the angle of the fingers remains quite like the original unbent position. Although it is hard to see, this type of bend relies upon the left hand pivoting off of the bone on that left hand just below the index finger, from the side of the guitar neck. In this case, I'm bending the A, or fifth string, up a whole step with the same three fingers as before.

Bending "away."

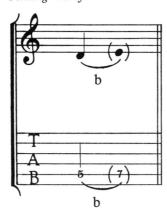

It is possible to bend a note solely with the index finger as long as this *pivoting* technique is employed. Here we see a relatively difficult half-step bend being played on the G string, fifth fret. Note that again, this note is being bent *away* from the player, a direction that will help give the strength that is required.

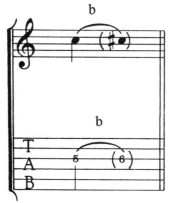

A one-finger bend "away."

One of the more intriguing forms of string bending is when you can combine a bent note with another stationary, fretted note, creating some interesting harmonies. The most common type is where a note is bent *toward* you on the B string while a note is held down on the high E string, on the same fret. In the following bend, I am using three fingers to push the B string, eighth fret, up a whole step, while my pinky holds down the eighth fret on the high E string. Make sure to pay close attention to the positioning of my fingers in this photograph.

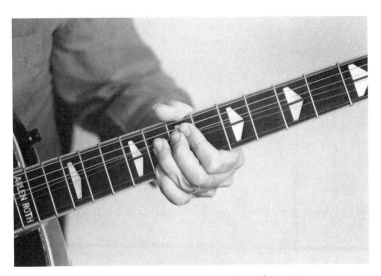

Three-fingered bend played in harmony with another note.

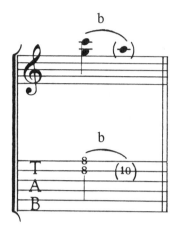

Please go over these positions and bends before you move on to the material in the next section. String bending is never an easy task, and on the acoustic guitar, with its heavier strings, presents more hurdles on the way toward proper technique and sound. For this reason, please be patient, and work hard at it. It will take some time, but you'll be well rewarded when it finally does sound the way you want it to!

Understanding String Bending as Substitution

One of the best and most effective ways of learning the theory of bent notes is to know what they would be substituting for should they be fretted normally. After all, one really couldn't expect to come up with new string-bending ideas and licks without being able to "visualize" what the bend is musically doing. To illustrate my point, here we see a two-note bend lick, illustrated first in "hammer-on" form. This is a good way to come to understand many bending licks, because the hammer-on is such a physical, movable technique on the guitar. In this way, you can then play the bend with a "mind's eye" picture of the position you're going to.

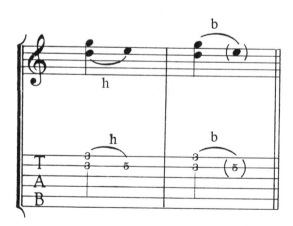

Licks and Exercises

I should mention here that this form of substitution was by far the most successful means by which I was able to achieve string-bending success. I was able to create literally hundreds of licks with substitution as my guide.

The act of hammering-on and then pulling-off can really act as a great source for string-bending licks using the bend and release principle. Here, for example, is a classic country hammer-on and pull-off lick transformed into a beautiful bend and release. Remember to keep that pinky firmly planted on the high E string so that the bend can achieve its proper independence.

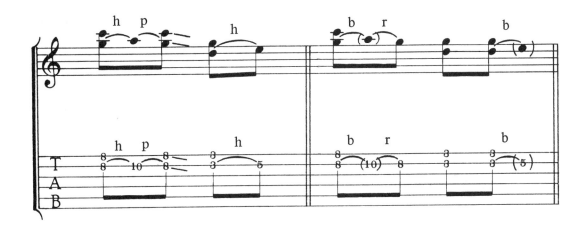

In this lick, an even more classic country ending, we see how the same position shifted to different frets creates new chord changes that actually exist within the structure of the bending lick. Make sure to play the slide I've indicated between positions; this will greatly enhance the "pedal-steel"–like sound of the string bending position. You'll see it here first in hammer-on form, then in its *substituted* bent form.

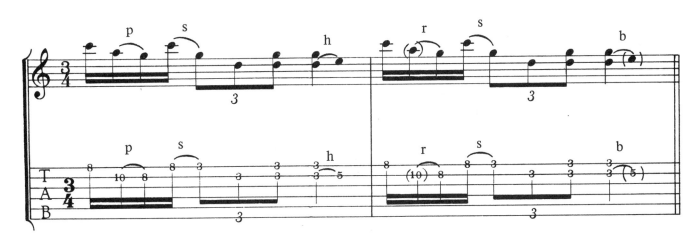

One string-bending position in which I like to employ the G string is the *suspended fourth*. In this particular case, the note is bent up to pitch *before* you play anything, picked, and *then* released. The G string, usually of the wound variety on acoustic guitars, makes bends of a length greater than a half step rather unlikely, not to mention that it's simply too painful! I should point out that *any* bend on this string would require the use of other fingers to help the bending finger along, and could not be sustained for very long.

In the following position, a partial index-finger barre is employed on the top two strings, while the second and third fingers carry the responsibility of the bend. The ability to bend a note up to pitch "silently" takes a great amount of trial and error before you can achieve the proper "feel" of just how far the string should be bent. In the course of this process, your fingers seem to develop preset "stops," with an inherent "sixth sense" of just how far to bend. As I said, it does take a lot of practice, but is surely one of the more rewarding guitar techniques.

In this lick, we play the first two notes, while the G string is already "silently" bent. Then, the G string suspended fourth is released while the first two notes are still vibrating. This creates a very pleasing full-chord *resolution*.

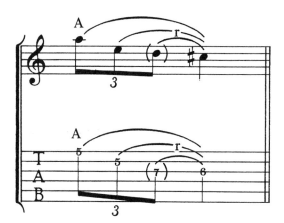

Perhaps the most difficult string-bending technique to master is to bend a note, play another on another string, and then change the note on that *unbent* string, while finally releasing the bend. I know this sounds like an awful lot, and it is! However, the real key to success with a lick of this type is once again the ability to *hold* the pitch of the bend while all this flurry of activity is going on around it. I can't emphasize enough the importance of using the other fingers to help the bend in cases such as this. Otherwise, all hope is lost.

Practice this little melodic lick slowly and carefully, trying to recreate the subtle nuances possible with this technique.

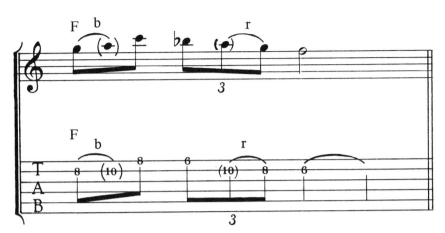

Now that we've basically covered all of the various types of string bending, it would be a good idea to go on to the following group of exercises. These are specially designed to show you the many string-bending possibilities that exist within the major pentatonic positions. Keep our preliminary exercise in mind when doing these, and of course, feel free to refer back to them should you reach a difficult juncture. Remember that the strength of your fingers and the correct positions are required in the proper execution of these licks.

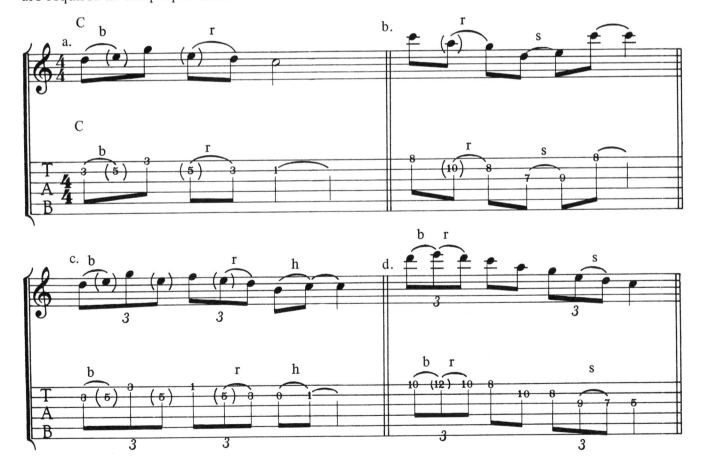

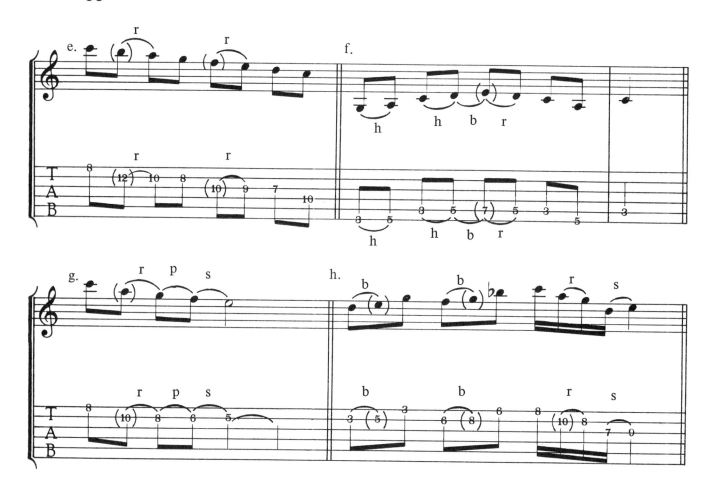

The following is a full-fledged country lead guitar piece that incorporates all of the bending licks and techniques I've been discussing heretofore. The melody and chord progression is reminiscent of the classic old-time country tune, "Wabash Cannonball," a melody that's in the blood of anyone familiar with traditional American folk and country music. Enjoy it!

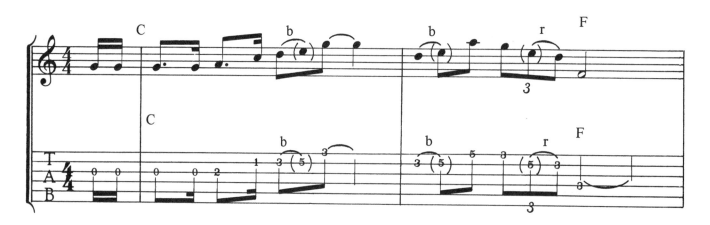

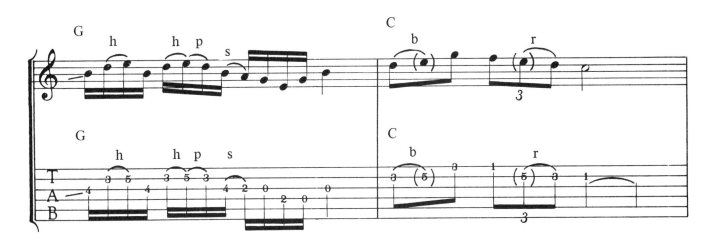

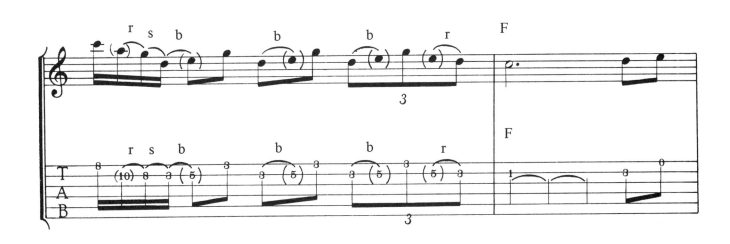

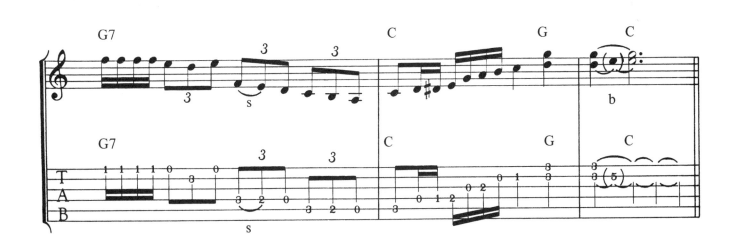

3

ACOUSTIC FLATPICKING: BLUES STYLES

Acoustic blues has always held a special place in the hearts of blues lovers, and represents the earlier form of this American art form. Blues began in the deep, rural South, and until the late 1940s and 1950s, when it moved north to Chicago, it remained largely an acoustic music form. Much of the music of guitarists like Son House, Robert Johnson, Tampa Red, Bukka White, Charlie Patton, Willie McTell, and countless others consisted of solo vocal and guitar performances. Group playing was not uncommon, however, and these acoustic bands would often include banjo, harmonica, washtub bass, mandolin, and sometimes even fiddle, although the latter has always been more associated with rural white country music than with blues. The guitar in acoustic blues shared both the rhythm and lead jobs, often incorporating fingerpicking techniques to achieve both of these techniques together. Another very major contribution to rural and later electric blues was slide, or bottleneck guitar, a technique we'll discuss at greater length in the section on Blues Fingerpicking in Chapter 4.

RHYTHM GUITAR

This is the essence of the driving pulse behind the blues. Blues is a decidedly rhythmic musical form, and its beat is one of unmistakable character. Without it, there would be no rhythm and blues, and no rock and roll.

The Shuffle

One of the most easily recognizable forms of blues rhythm guitar playing is called the "shuffle." This is a very popular form of the blues and owes its name to the fact that the measure, rather than consisting of eight uniform eighth notes, is actually comprised of four groups of triplets, translated as eighth notes.

To illustrate how this shuffle feel looks in a rhythmic sense, study the following diagrams, which show the measure broken into triplets and "shuffle" eighth notes.

I (Tonic)	IV	V
E	A	B
F	B♭	C
F♯ or G♭	B C♭	C♯ D♭
G	C	D
A♭	D♭	E♭
A	D	E
B♭	E♭	F
B	E	F♯
C	F	G
D♭	G♭	A♭
D	G	A
E♭	A♭	B♭

Diagram 6. I–IV–V Chords

The I–IV–V Progressions

The blues form, although consisting of an endless array of chord patterns, is most exemplified by the 12-bar, I–IV–V variety. This numerical form of labeling chord progressions enables us to communicate familiar changes without needing to actually mention the key or the name of the chord. The numbers are derived from the number of notes that the chord is away from the tonic in the major scale. For example, a I–II–III–IV–V progression in the key of E would be E, F♯, G♯, A, B. Diagram 6 provides a list of all the keys and their IV and V chords as a reference chart.

The Twelve-Bar Blues

Here is how the 12-bar blues looks. This is the most classic form of the blues, and it's written out here for the key of E, with both chord names and numerical values.

The 12-Bar Blues

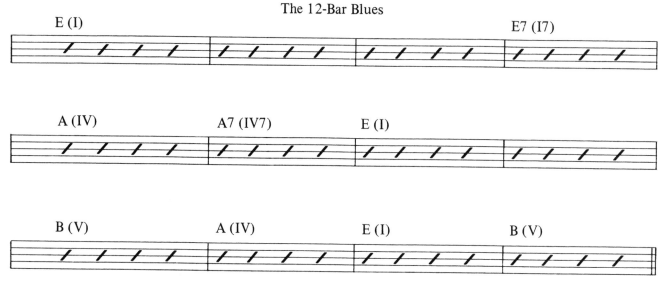

The Turnaround

The *turnaround* is a big part of blues music, and is the musical passage during the final two measures of a 12-bar blues that actually serves to "turn the song around" again and bring it back to the beginning. Here again is the 12-bar blues in E with the addition of the turnaround.

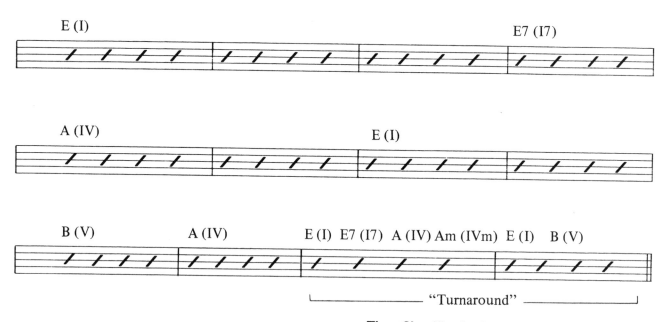

The Shuffle Lick

In the shuffle rhythm guitar lick, the most common position is to play only the two bottom-most notes of the chord—providing, however, that these notes are the root and the fifth. To achieve these positions we must use notes from the E and A chord forms, both open and closed, or barred. In this first exercise, we see the easiest form of the shuffle. We are playing *all* open positions, for the A, D, and E chords, and the lick simply shifts from one pair of strings to another. Remember to keep your picking accurate, or you could end up with a lot of unwanted open strings ringing.

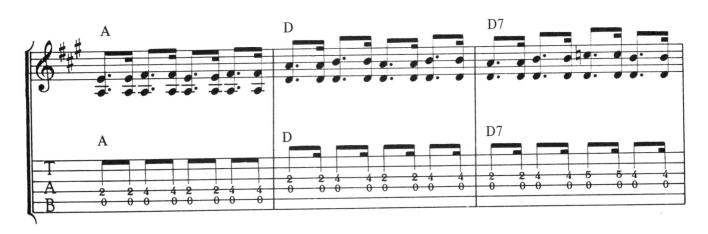

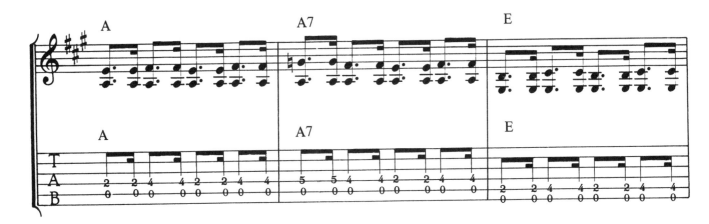

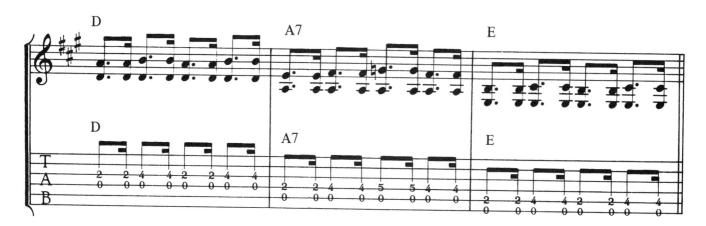

This shuffle, for the key of E, uses open positions for both the E and A chords, but must transfer to a partial usage of the A barre form of B. This requires a bit more stretching than we've been accustomed to, particularly because we are making the stretch on the lower, wider frets. For the B-shuffle lick, the first and third fingers play the first two notes. Then, the index finger remains on the second fret of the A string while the pinky reaches to play the sixth fret on the D.

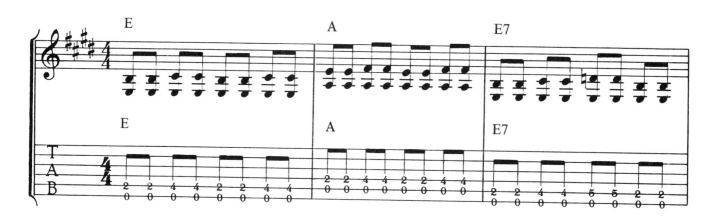

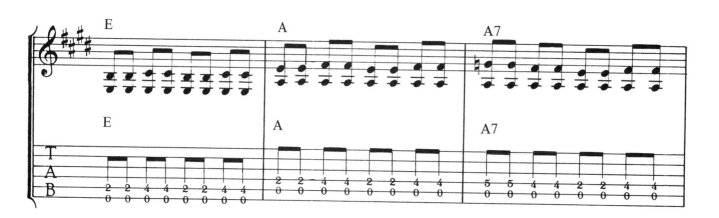

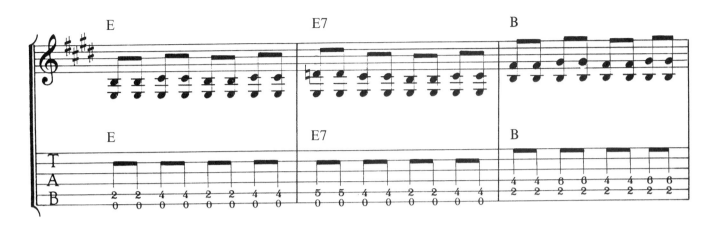

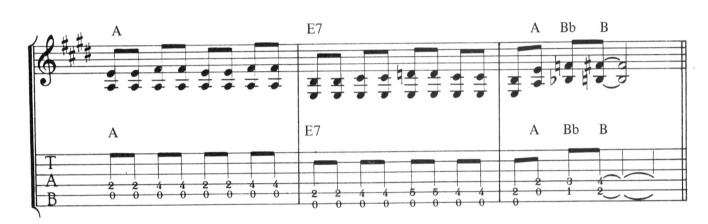

As a more difficult and challenging exercise, I've written here the shuffle for G, using solely partial forms of the "closed" barre positions of G, C, and D. Please remember to keep those left-hand stretches consistent.

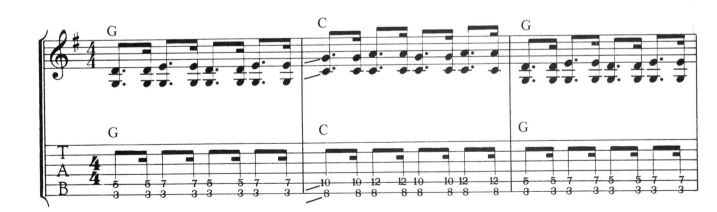

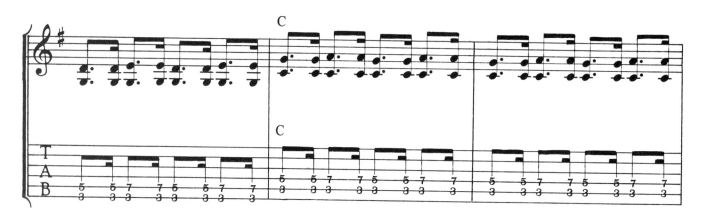

The Alternating Shuffle

The "alternating" shuffle has a nice roll-along kind of feeling, and requires some different, though not necessarily more difficult, flatpicking than in the previous exercises.

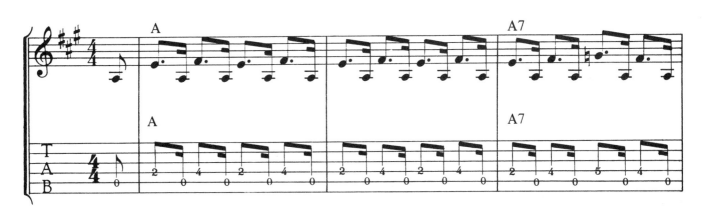

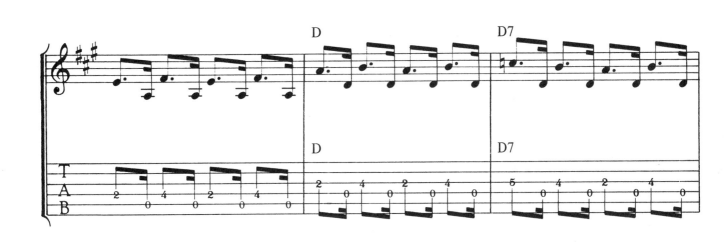

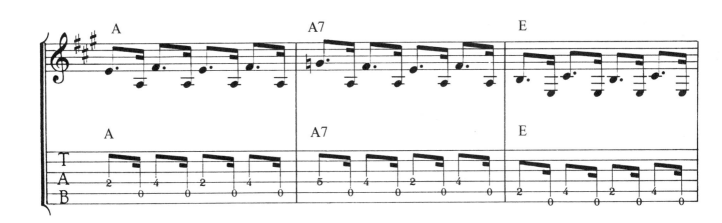

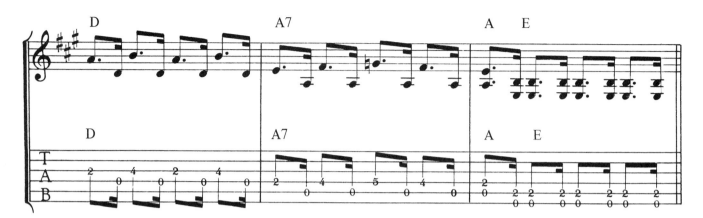

The Harmony Shuffle

Another interesting form of blues rhythm guitar is what I call the "harmony" shuffle. In this position, two notes rather than one are simultaneously in harmony with each other. In fact, the second harmonized part of the lick is actually the IV chord of the key in which you're playing, with the tonic root as a bass note. In the case of this first position for E, we are alternating between an E and an A chord, and the finger that is fretting the A string must also lightly touch the D string to *damp* it out. Note that the third position of the shuffle, E7, is a repetition of the first part, merely moved up the neck three frets, or a step and a half.

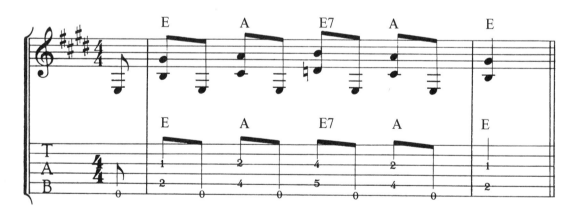

This shuffle position in the key of A necessitates a partial index-finger barre on the D, G, and B strings to create a full A chord. This forms a convenient base for the second chord position to be placed upon. This is a very useful technique for both lead and rhythm work, and we'll see it more often as the book progresses.

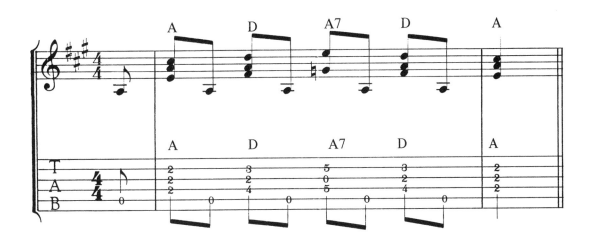

Physically speaking, the G position of the harmony shuffle is the same as the A, only moved two frets down to the open strings. The major difference is that we need the third finger to maintain the bass G notes for the first two chords, but when we play the third, G7, we must quickly *switch* fingers so the index now plays the low G note. This will take some getting used to before the transition can be made smoothly enough to sound like it never occurred.

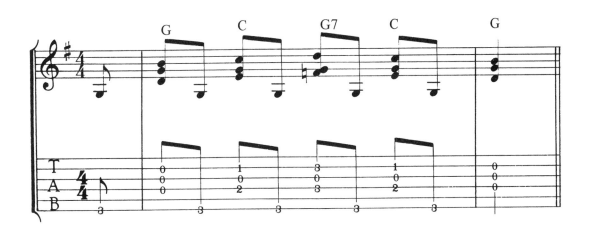

In the D position, we again see the importance of partial barres as played by the index finger. In the case of the D chord, we can now play it with two fingers rather than the standard three by creating a barre at the second fret, as in the next photo.

In the second chord of the lick, our index finger barres only the top *two* strings while our second finger comes over to play the fourth fret on the G string. The third chord, D7, requires three fingers.

Open D chord using index finger barre.

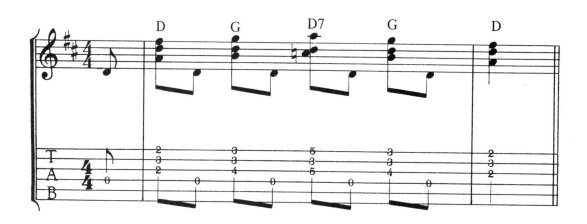

The following piece is a 12-bar blues in the key of D that demonstrates how you can switch from one open-harmony shuffle position to another. Note the placement of the seventh chords and their different characteristics.

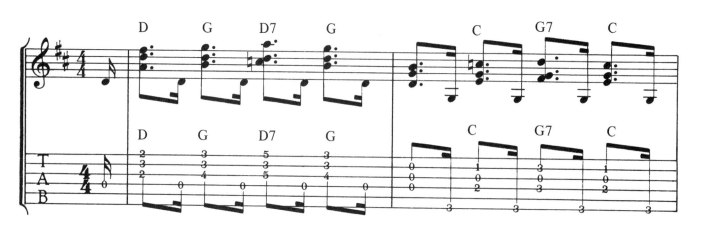

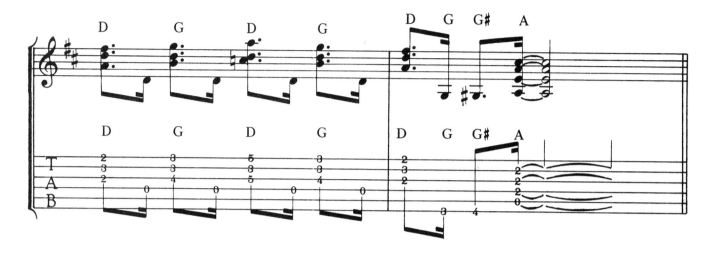

Turnaround Licks

Previously, I mentioned the point at the end of the 12-bar blues that serves as the turnaround. This particular musical moment has given birth to countless licks that can become quite an interesting and important part of the blues guitarist's vocabulary. As you'll see, they are, for the most part, quite easy to execute compared to other single-note passages. This is because they frequently involve repetitions of the same note groupings, moving downward one fret at a time. For example, if you were playing the harmony shuffle for E, you could create a turnaround lick from the very same position you were playing in, as in this triplet run. Be sure to use alternating picking strokes for this kind of repetitive run.

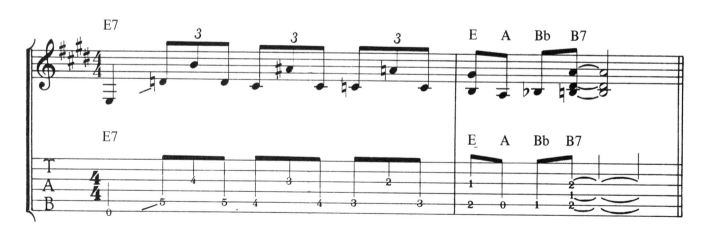

Even if you are primarily playing rhythm guitar, the turnaround lick provides a nice, lead-guitar-like change of pace from the comparatively mundane chord work. Here are a large group of similar triplet-note turnaround licks, written for the key of E. Try to fit them in at the end of playing a 12-bar blues progression, as well as *transposing* them to other keys and positions.

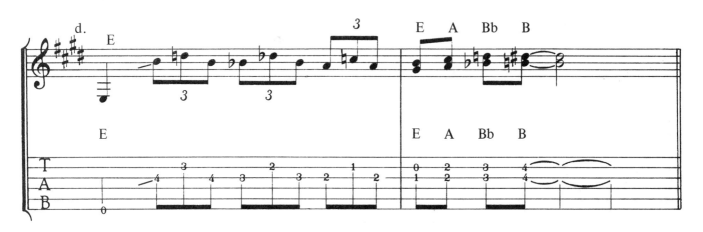

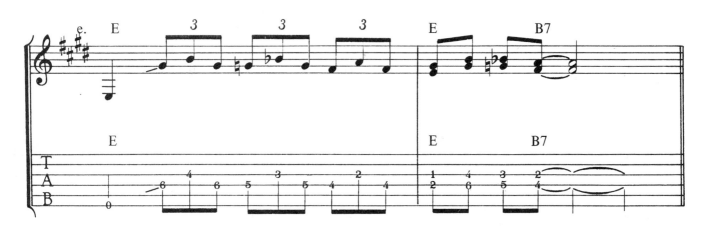

Walking Bass Lines

You've probably noticed in blues and rock music a kind of moving, or "walking" line often played by the bass, or on the lower keys of the piano. In early blues and boogie-woogie, particularly of the solo, one-man variety, the guitarist would often play this line as an accompaniment to the vocal line, or as part of the solo. This kind of playing can really be a lot of fun, and is a nice little trick to have in your repertoire.

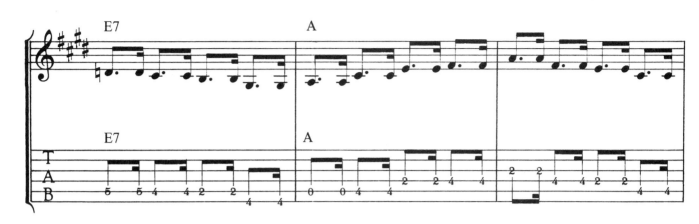

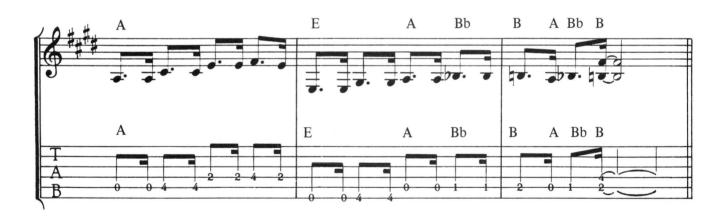

This first and very common form of the walking bass line accurately follows the shuffle pattern. Try to play it with an upbeat tempo.

If you break up the straight shuffle pattern a bit, you can give the walking bass lick more character, as exemplified in the following exercise.

Learning to "Squeeze" the Chords

The only way to truly develop more complex rhythm guitar patterns is to use the left hand to damp and "squeeze" the chords at the right times. The easiest way in which to visualize this is to have the chord touching the strings, but *not* actually depressing the notes until called upon to do so. In this way, you feel as if the chord lies right beneath your fingers, just waiting to be played! Clearly, the advantage in this technique is that the right hand can maintain some rather complex rhythmic patterns, while the left hand plays the dual roles of both damping and playing.

When describing this technique to students, I often liken it to being a drummer. After all, the strings of the guitar have bass or treble tones, and when damped they actually can resemble the various sounds of the drum kit. Taking it one step further, you can equate these sounds specifically to the bass drum, snare, and even the high hat. Before we go on to playing, I would like you to try some of these purely rhythmic exercises by covering the strings with your left hand, and using the pick to create these drum-like patterns.

In this first pattern, we are making a very clear distinction between the bass and treble of the guitar. In fact, beneath the music I've written what would be the drum set's counterpart. Please accent the notes that correspond to the *snare.* These are the accented *backbeats* of the measure, occurring on beats two and four. The bass drum is represented by the lowest strings, while the highest are the treble. The snare, for the backbeats, is in the mid-range.

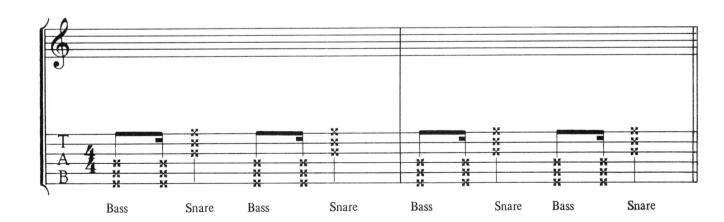

This next rhythm exercise has the same backbeat accents as before, only now there are some more little complex patterns incorporated into the right-hand movement. These resemble the time-keeping high-hat cymbal of the drumset, and lend a great deal more subtlety to the playing. In actuality, the more complex these patterns become, the easier they should be to play. This is due to the fact that the more notes you must play, the more relaxed your wrist must be. If it seems to be getting more and more difficult for you, that should be a good tip-off to you that your wrist isn't quite relaxed enough.

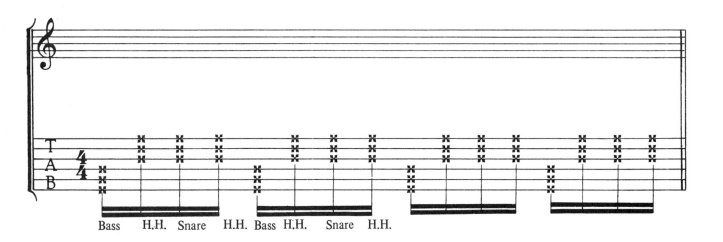

Bass H.H. Snare H.H. Bass H.H. Snare H.H.

These patterns for the C7 position of E7 show how the rhythmic exercises we've been practicing sound with chords. In place of the standard use of rests, I've written out the drum-like, damped patterns that exist between the fretted chords. Be sure to have them ready to play, and to then "squeeze" them at the appropriate times.

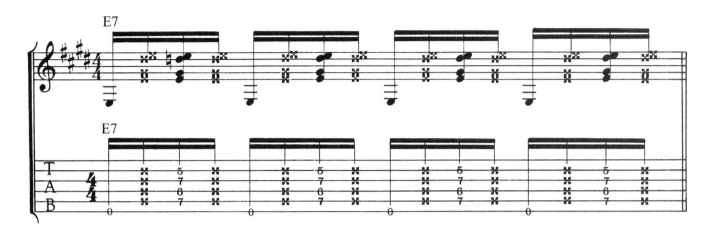

This next pattern is among my all-time favorites, especially for laying down a good rhythm part to jam with. It's based upon a rhythmic feel closely related to gospel music, and it's played in both half-time and double-time patterns. The difference between them lies in the backbeat, with the half time having two per measure, and the double time having four. Here is the first, with a really hard-driving feeling to it. Once again, take note of the drum parts, and be sure to relax into them before starting to squeeze the chords.

Now, in the gospel-like rhythm part, we are employing two very useful and effective left-hand techniques. First, for the A chord, we're using a partial barre across the D, G, and B strings in tandem with the open A string to create an interesting voicing. Our second finger will create the hammer-on onto our major third to finish the chord, and then another quick partial barre across the seventh fret with our ring finger will form the D chord.

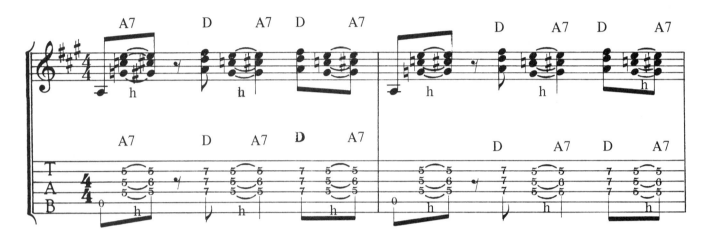

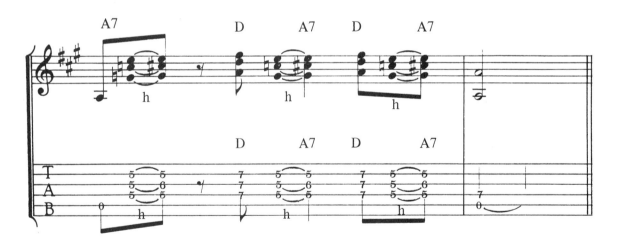

This is the "double-time" version of the gospel rhythm lick, and basically takes the previous pattern and divides all of its elements in half. This pattern will *seem* faster, even though its tempo is basically the same as before. The right hand must make its moves quite a bit faster here, so you're well advised to take this exercise slowly at first, speeding up as your confidence increases.

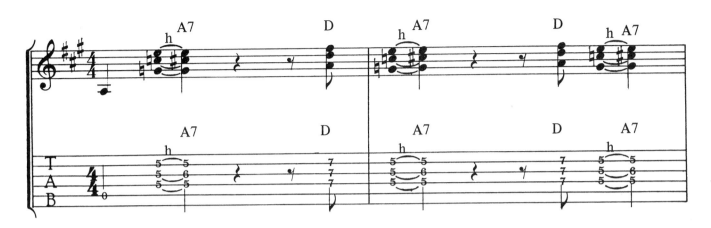

LEAD BLUES GUITAR

The art of lead guitar, particularly in the blues idiom, is generally thought of as an electric guitar technique. Of course, the electric guitar, with its lighter strings, more readily lends itself to all of the bluesy bending required. Still, you'll find that the acoustic guitar certainly has a lot to offer.

Having first developed over a long period of time as an electric guitarist, I like to think of my understanding of the acoustic blues guitar as a true blend of both electric and acoustic techniques. Because I developed this way, I became very expressive on the electric guitar first, while never letting the acoustic guitar, with its heavier strings, quieter tone, and higher action, stand in my way. This was a good thing, because the "tension" of one style's clash with another created something new for me, with its own special language. In this same way, if you're first picking up the acoustic after playing electric for quite some time, you should not feel intimidated by the acoustic guitar's new set of demands. Rather, you should work to put them to use for *you*, and to help shape your own unique style.

Blues Scale No. 1

This first position of the blues scale for open E is, as you'll notice in all of these scales, the *same* pentatonic scale we worked with back in Chapter 2, on Country/Folk Styles. The same note relationships exist, but the entire scale is now moved *up* a step and a half from the "country" position. It's also now referred to as the *minor* pentatonic because it contains the minor third and the seventh of the chord, both of which are notes in the true minor scale. Due to these major and minor relationships, we see that the major pentatonic for one chord becomes the minor, or blues pentatonic, for its *relative minor* chord. In other words, the C major pentatonic scale becomes the *blues* scale for A minor. The notes remain the same, while the root changes; therefore, different notes become important, and of course, change roles dramatically.

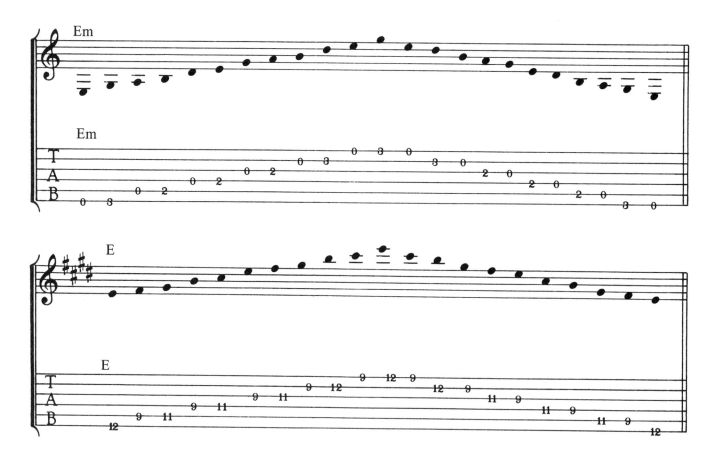

Passing Notes

The "passing" notes we saw earlier in the country section were flatted thirds. Now, within the blues form of the pentatonic, these same passing notes become the *flatted fifths*. This is a true "blue" note, and finds itself in many a blues lick. Here is how the flatted fifths fit into the first-position blues scale.

When moving this blues position up the neck to other keys, I prefer dropping down a whole step on the A string to play the second note of the scale. This is not the typical way in which this scale is generally taught, but I feel that having the first finger on the minor third rather than the third or fourth finger up on the low E string serves to better open up the position for creativity. Here is this form of the scale in the key of G.

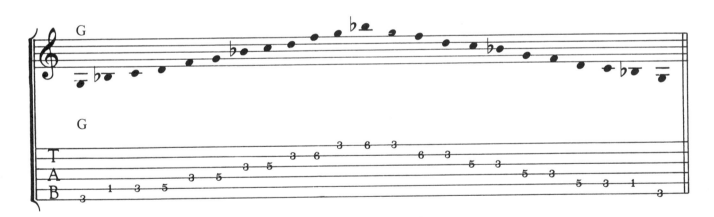

For the passing notes, or flatted fifths of this position, it would be advisable to use your third finger to "walk" up chromatically between the third and fifth frets on the A string. This will increase your mobility between two crucial positions, and give you more freedom when working within this and other scales.

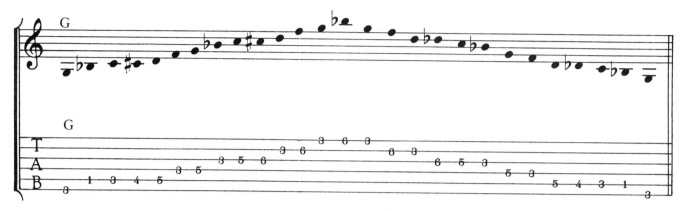

Various Licks

The flatted fifths often act as an inegral part of many blues licks, and the ones that do include this note are of a particular character. In addition to string bending, which we will work into blues playing shortly, these licks often use pull-offs, hammer-pulls, or slides as additions to this flatted fifth style. The following lick, in both the open E and closed G positions, shows the straight pull-off style. When playing this piece, it's important to have the fingers that are to be playing below the pull-off ready on each of their respective frets. This will aid greatly in proper execution of pull-offs.

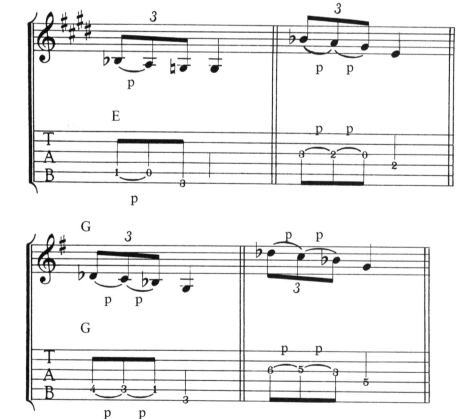

Now, in a more complex and musically interesting style, we use the same position and notes; but by adding an extra hammer-on at the beginning, we create a lick that has an extended sound with more flair than the previous way of playing it. Take special care in the fingering of this one, because you'll actually be creating *four* individual notes with one stroke of the pick!

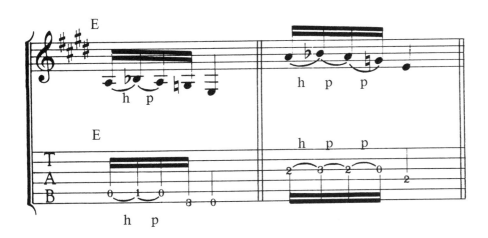

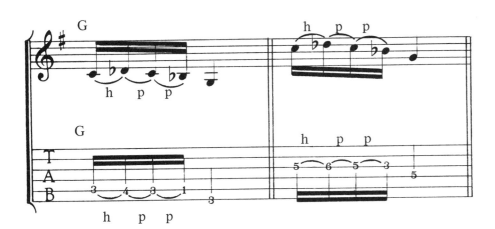

By using a back-and-forth *slide* between two notes to create three, we can play it with fewer fingers and a slightly quicker sound. As we can see in the first part of the closed G position, this is particularly useful when playing it on the relatively low A string. This helps to avoid any unnecessary, difficult stretches.

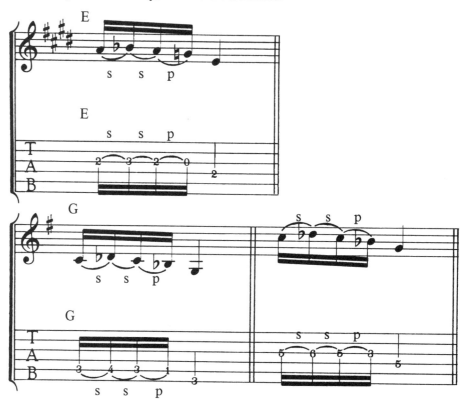

The following two groups of licks, for the open and closed positions of the first blues scale, really show you some of the countless improvisational possibilities that are available. Try to pay close attention to the "phrasing" of these note groupings, for this is what makes them licks and not simply random notes. Also take note of the extensive use of left-hand techniques such as hammer-ons, pull-offs, and slides.

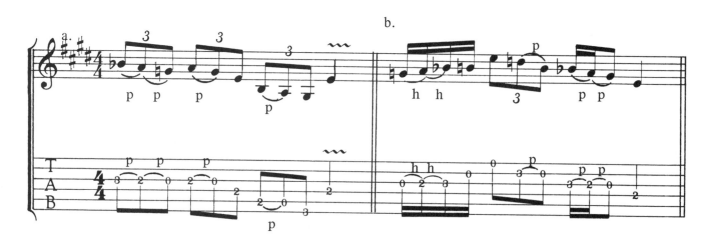

c.

d.

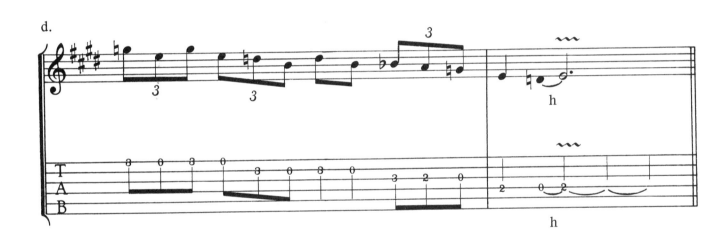

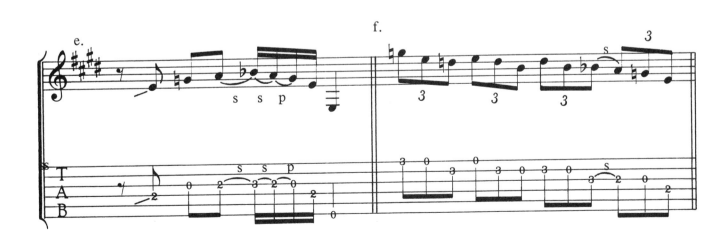

g.

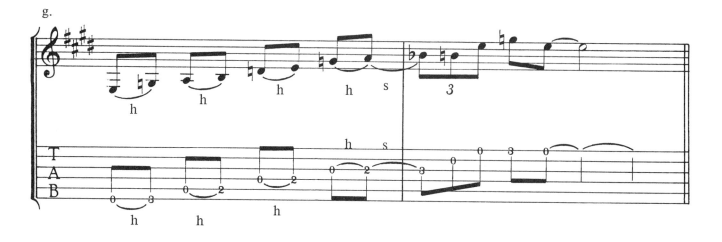

h.

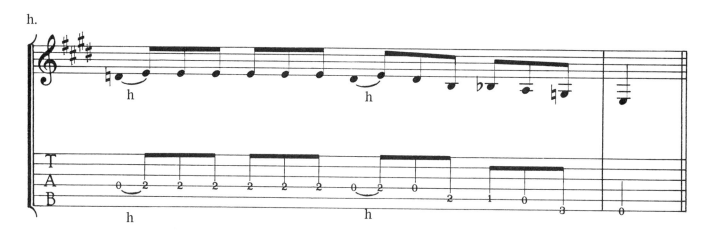

i.

j.

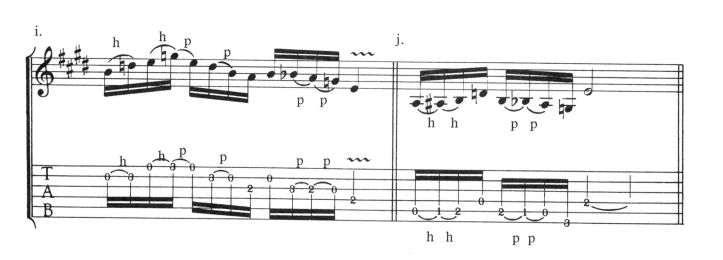

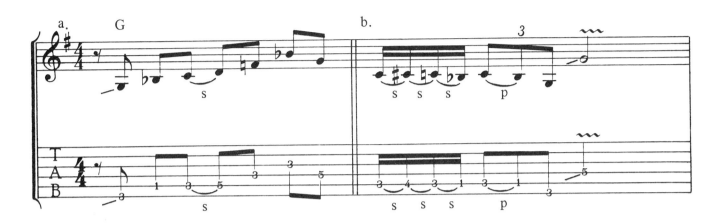

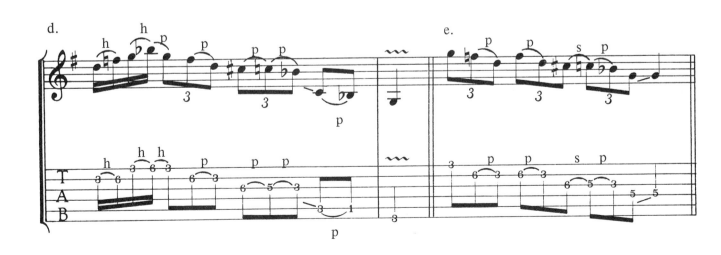

f.

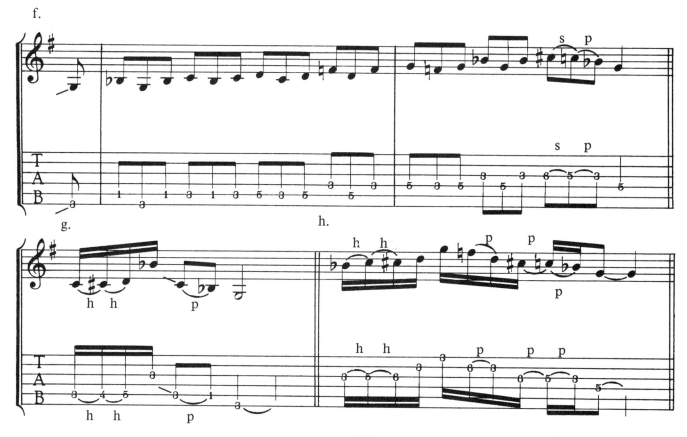

g.   h.

Blues Scale No. 2

The unique quality of this particular scale is that it takes the previous one and opens it up, adding a higher position on top. This particular area of the fretboard, encircled in the scales that follow for easy recognition, plays host to the vast majority of improvisational blues lead work. Because we are now adding length to the scale, we are also adding higher notes and far more possibilities to your playing. To get an initial idea of how this blues scale should feel, I've written it here for the open E and closed G positions.

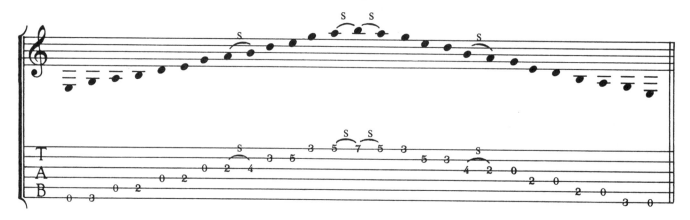

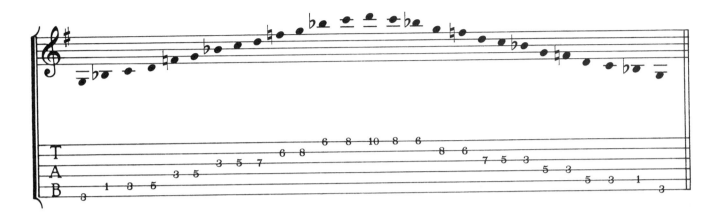

Sliding from the fourth to the fifth of this scale, now in three locations, helps you to move much more quickly from one position to the next. In the case of this scale, I would recommend using the third finger for the slide on the A string, and the second finger for the slides that lie on the G and high E.

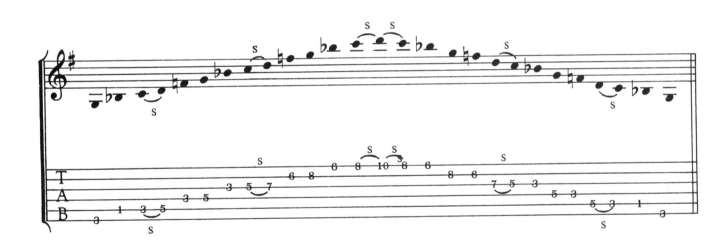

Here is a form of this scale I like to give students to work on because it makes a unique use of not only the slides, but of partial barreing as well. In the case of the two barre positions, we are really playing the same licks, only one full octave apart. The positioning is different, but the notes remain the same. In addition, it would be a good practice to use the barre only for the actual duration of the notes that you *are* barreing. In this way, you'll be releasing the barre when it is really no longer needed, and you won't overwork your poor left hand!

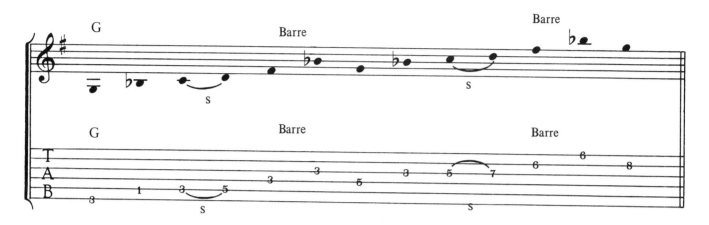

Incorporating Hammer-ons and Pull-offs

Where hammer-ons and pull-offs are concerned, they can transform this scale into some dazzling spectacles of technique and speed! With the use of well-placed right- and left-hand techniques, we can transform this scale into something that "speaks" unlike the way most scales tend to just "sit there."

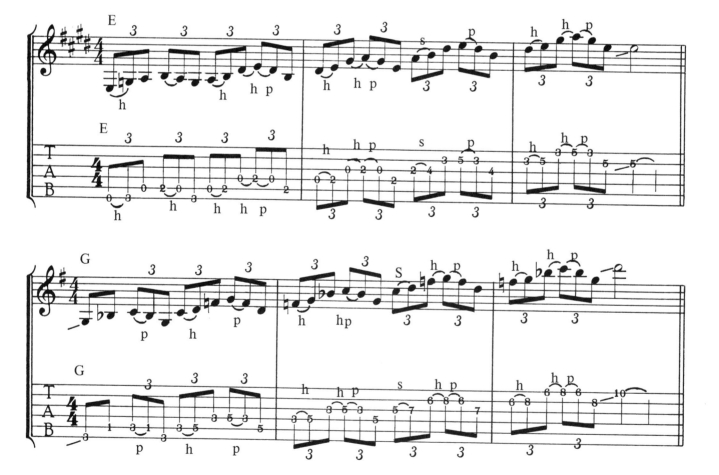

Various Licks

The licks available to you within this position are endless, but I thought I'd spark some ideas of your own with this assortment. Again, pay close attention to the technical side of things, such as hammer-ons, pull-offs, and slides, and you'll receive the most from these licks. Also, try to keep your shifts from one position to another as smooth as possible. This is when the licks will really take on special character.

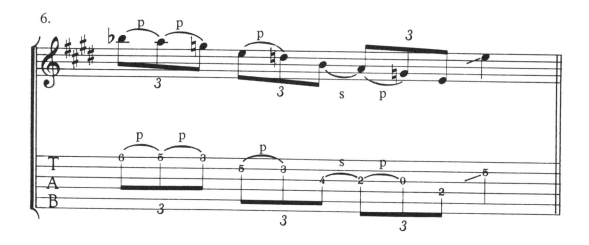

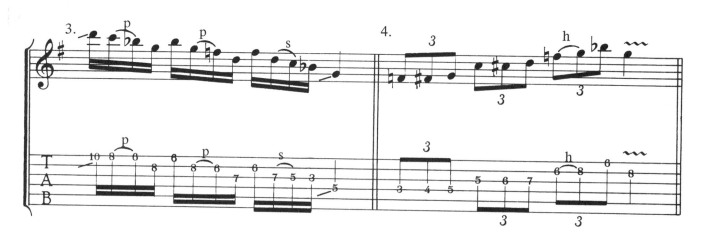

Blues Scale No. 3

With this position, we are changing things rather drastically by moving the whole position over one string. It's really not as much of a serious change as you might think, though. After all, we're still playing a blues scale, and the note relationships remain the same. As a means of showing you the contrast of this position, it's written here for the key of E, with the first note lying on the seventh fret of the A string. This movement of all the notes over one string marks a radical departure from our previous blues scales, and you'll see that it possesses an entirely new texture and tonality.

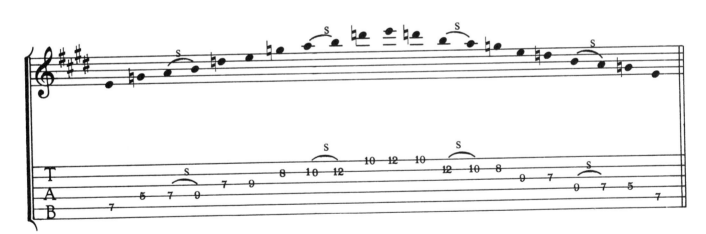

As you can see in the following group of runs, the notes are still the same, but the positions and their relationships to the root are quite different. Note how we never play above the highest E, making all the licks seem to have a "threshold" under which they remain.

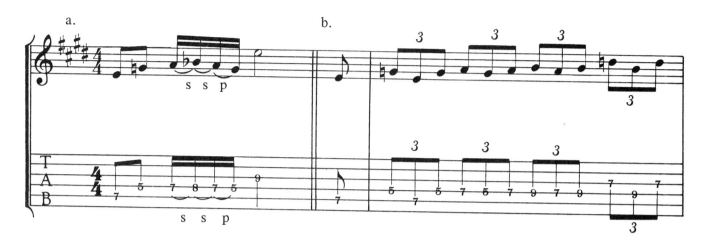

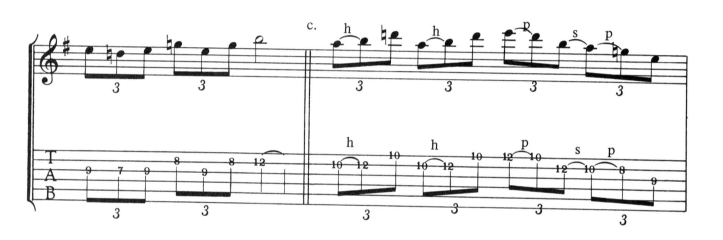

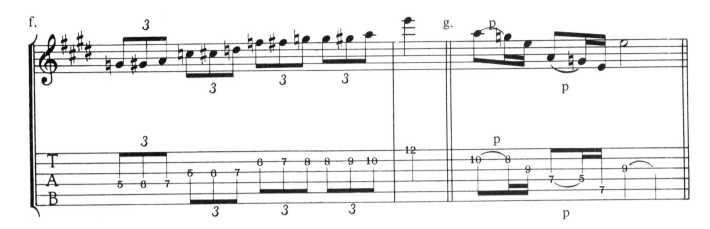

STRING BENDING—BLUES STYLE

With the art of string bending, I feel that we are exploring the nitty-gritty of guitar as a means of expression. Bending a string, or altering its pitch without changing the fret, is perhaps the one technique that gives the guitar its most "vocal" quality. I might add that pianists can get fairly frustrated and envious when guitarists bend strings, because this is the one limitation of *their* instrument! (Unless they reach into the main part of the piano and start bending there, or have one of the new synthesizers that electronically bends tones.) In any event, electric guitars, with their lighter strings, particularly the unwound G, make string bending a much more viable technique. Indeed, they are far more associated with this fine art than their acoustic cousins. However, the acoustic guitar is, I feel, a wonderful vehicle for blues string bending, and must be explored if you expect to become the "complete acoustic guitarist."

The majority of acoustic guitars are equipped to handle string sets that include a wound G or third string. I would advise not going over a *light* gauge at all if you expect to do any bending, for obvious reasons. Even though the G string is wound, it isn't to be avoided in the bending process, and you'll find that the low E, A, B, and high E strings are *very* conducive to bending. The D string is rather stiff, but still merits a good deal of attention.

Back in Chapter 2 on Country/Folk Styles, we discussed the actual physical act of string bending, so it would be advisable to go back and review any questionable techniques before jumping ahead in this section.

The blues is probably where string bending got its start. In the early days of acoustic blues, many of these "blues" or discordant notes were achieved by a slight "slurring" of the rather heavy strings that were the norm of the time. Perhaps the early influence of the Hawaiian players, with their sliding notes, helped give birth to string bending as an emulation of this sound. In fact, B. B. King, one of the greatest blues benders of all time, attributes his first experiments as a replacement to an unsuccessful attempt at trying to sound like his cousin Bukka White, the great slide guitarist. Whatever its origins, string bending is still the most "vocal" aspect of slide playing, both acoustic and electric.

Bending With Vibrato

Blues bends are rarely played without a healthy dose of *vibrato* thrown in, which serves to further add to that vocal quality. As with singing, they are often most effective when used after the note reaches its final pitch.

A bend toward you is a difficult technique to combine with vibrato, yet is probably the most common. When creating this kind of vibrato, you must actually release and rebend the string back up to pitch for each beat of the wavering vibrato. This will be rather difficult at first, and I can safely predict that you're likely to have a hard time keeping the note up to pitch. However, your fingers will get used to it after awhile. Keep in mind that this is one of the most difficult *and* rewarding things you'll *ever* have to master on the instrument! So please don't get too discouraged.

In this first bend, try a slow, deliberate vibrato. It's very important to maintain an even pulse to the vibrato, and each waver should be of equal length and pitch. Be sure not to release the bend too much, or else it will sound like a drop to a half step below.

In the case of a bend that is away from you, the vibrato should come as a result of an equal and rhythmic *pivoting* motion. As in all vibratos and bends, this should be from the lowest part of the side of the forefinger, at the side of the neck. The photo below the next music exercise illustrates the proper position. The same pivoting technique applies to index finger bends, or to notes that are not bent at all. The hand must be totally committed to the bending process, and the pivoting point is the only place on the neck, besides the fret, that receives strong pressure.

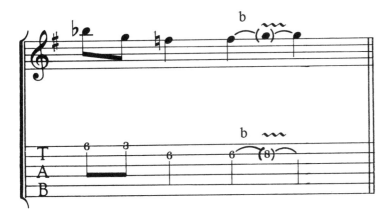

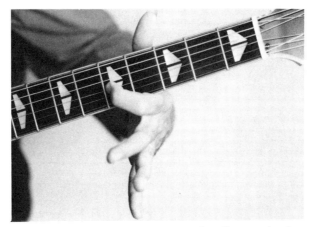

Proper index-finger pivoting position for vibrato or bend.

The Scales—What Notes are Bent?

When you choose a note to be bent, you are making a musical decision that will either show your knowledge or expose your weaknesses to the discerning listener. When many guitarists are learning to bend, they merely start bending every note they can find, rather than making the bend make sense musically and harmonically. This is certainly fine for a developing technique, but eventually it must reflect a developed ear, as well.

In the following blues scale for G, I've circled the notes that are bent most often. The notes they're bent to are the very same notes that follow them in the scale.

In this next scale, the notes in circles are the notes that should be bent a half step as well as a whole. These mostly involve the passing notes between the fourth and the fifth of the scale, the true "blue" notes we talked of earlier.

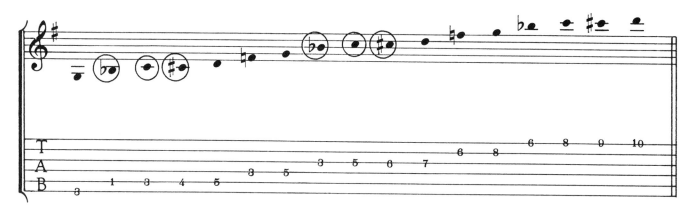

Licks and Exercises

The collection of licks that follows shows some of the bending experiments within the blues scales. Again, *phrasing* is the key element

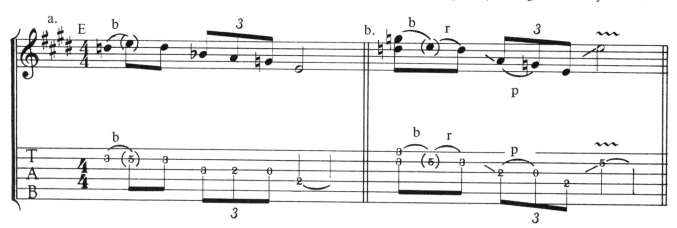

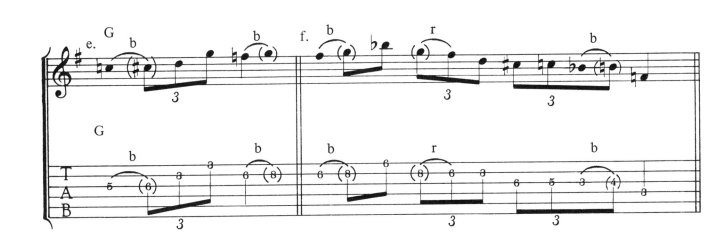

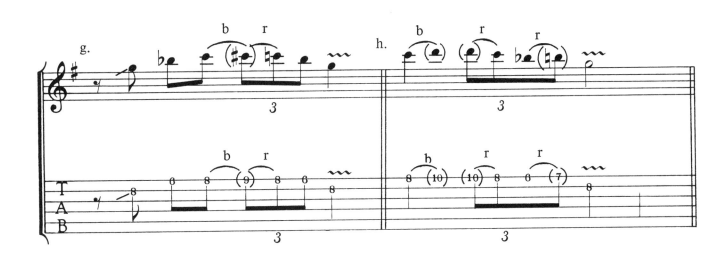

102

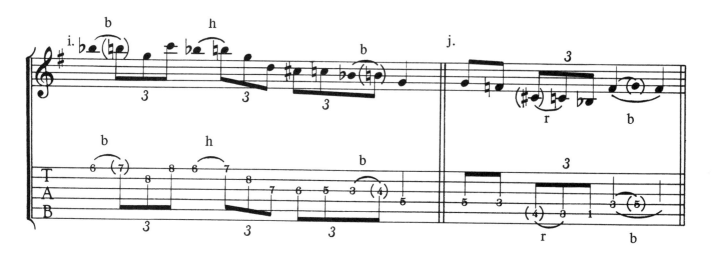

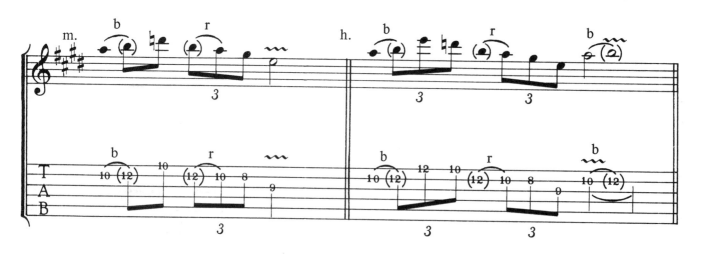

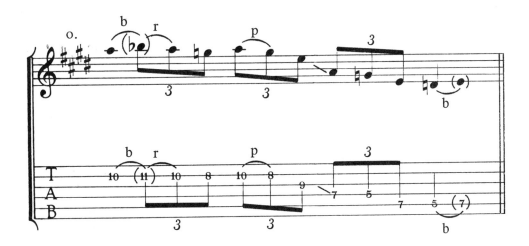

to watch for. Make sure to bend to the proper pitch. If these notes are somewhat unclear to you, first play the notes in parentheses as fretted notes, and then try to make the bend reach that pitch. This will serve to train your ear for more accurate bending, and someday you'll be able to pick up the guitar and "silently" bend to a note *before* it is actually sounded. It's certainly something to aim for.

Acoustic Blues Solos

The acoustic guitar is a marvelous instrument for solo work, and whether played alone or in a band context, the results can be equally rewarding. This first piece, written to be played in a solo situation, incorporates both rhythm and lead styles. I feel this is an important exercise, not only for getting around quickly on the instrument, but because acoustic guitar can make such a wonderful solo musical statement. It's great to be able to sit around and bounce rhythm and lead off one another, and it makes the guitarist realize just how self-sufficient he or she really can be.

Played in the shuffle feel, it's very important to land right on the proper downbeats in this next piece.

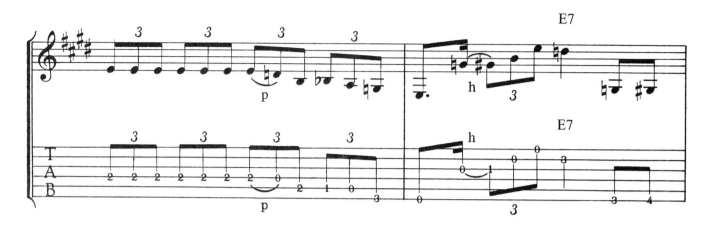

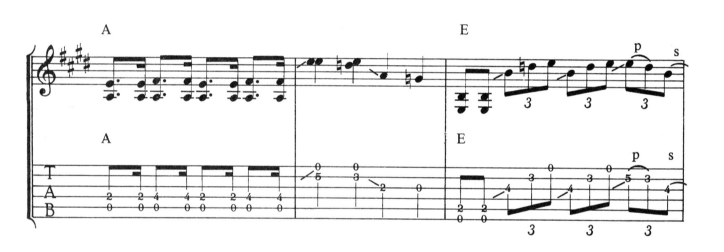

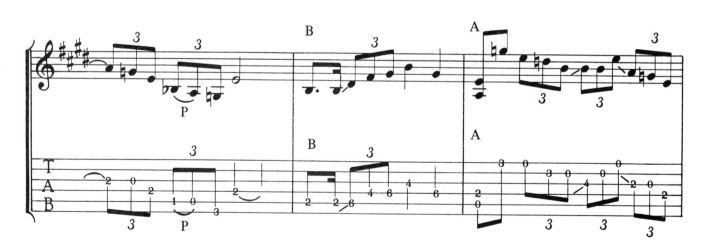

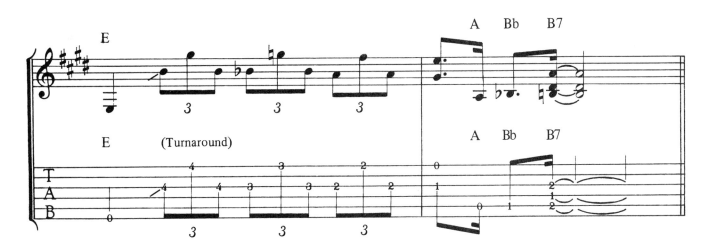

The next solo exercise deals strictly with the lead approach within the open E position. Take special note as to how the choice of notes within and outside the scale helps define the particular chord change over which you're playing.

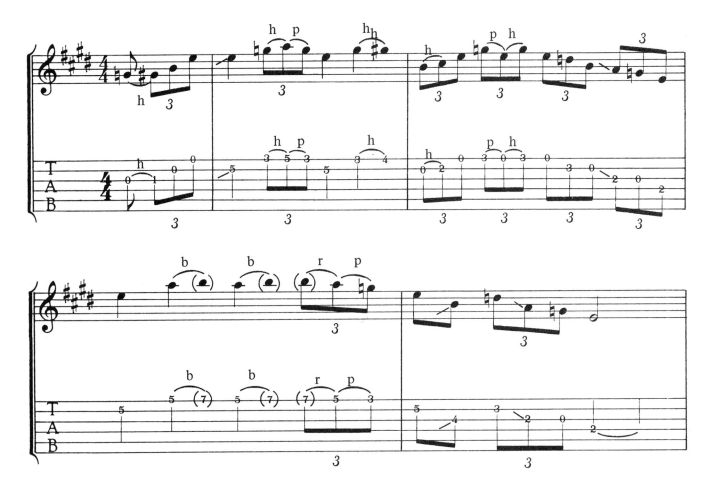

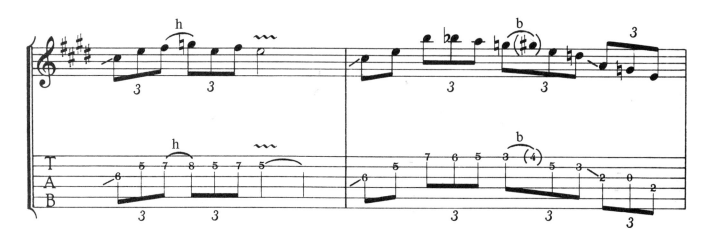

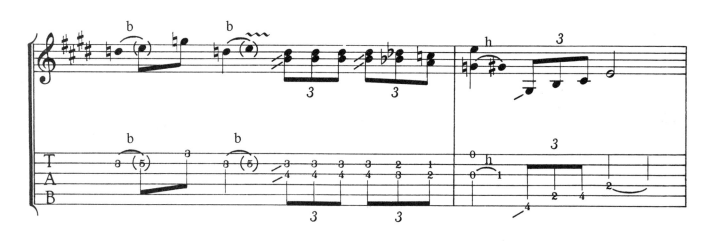

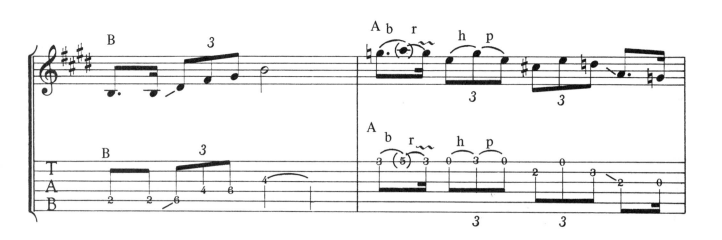

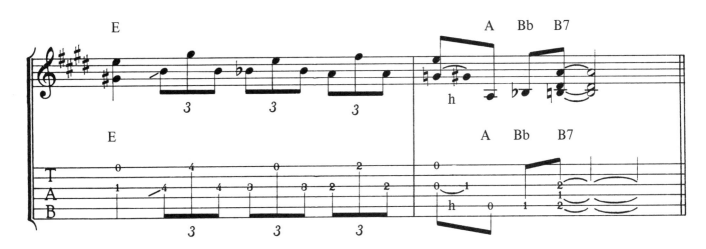

This third piece is a bit more elusive, because it's in the *closed* position of G, and uses no convenient open strings. You must, therefore, be careful about your left-hand fingering and movement because every note is being created by that hand. Notice how the turnaround is a much freer style of lick, far more within proper context than the more predictable turnarounds we've been playing.

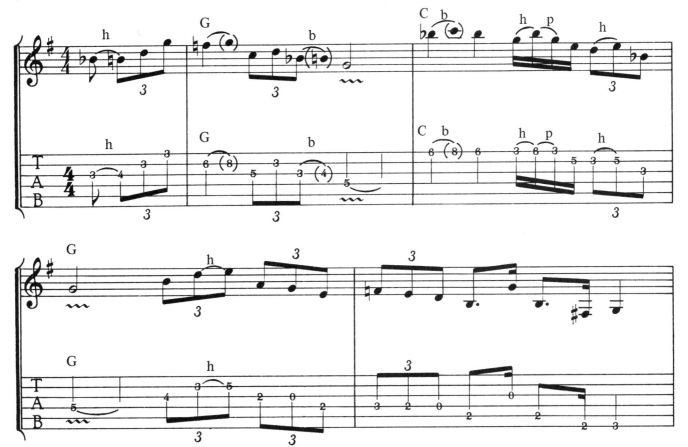

E98

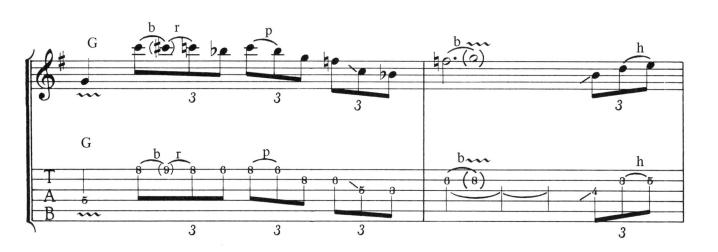

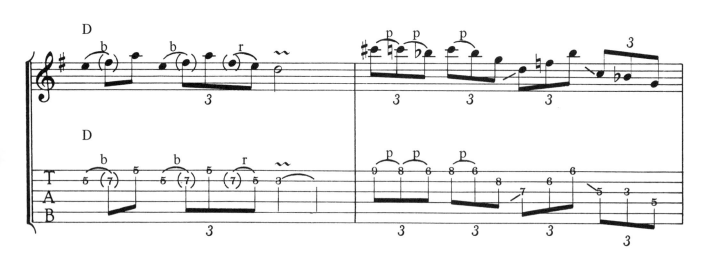

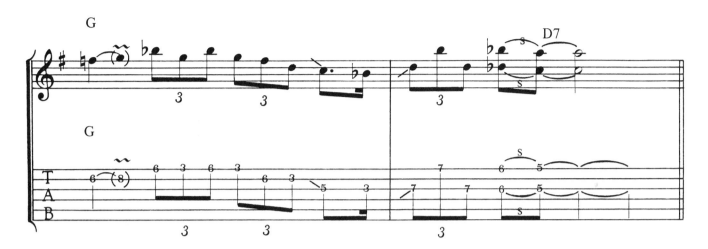

ACOUSTIC FINGERPICKING

As far as self-sufficiency goes, fingerpicking surely tops the list. When it comes to the solo styles of classical, flamenco, country, blues, bottleneck, folk, and ragtime, fingerpicking is the one absolute essential. This is due to the split-sound nature of the fingerpicking style. The independence that exists between the thumb and other fingers gives you the opportunity to have total control over the full range your guitar has to offer. Most players utilize a thumb and two finger technique, but why leave out the ring finger?! The ability to play four notes at once or independently is so intriguing, it's just a shame if any teacher encourages the use of only three fingers! Well, whether I'm undoing that damage, or starting you fresh, I'm sure you'll be glad when you know you can use all of these fingers.

The two following photos show the proper right-hand position for fingerpicking. The first shows the "ready" position, with the top three

The "ready" position for fingerpicking.

strings held ready to be played by the index, middle, and ring fingers. The thumb is shown ready to pluck the low E.

This next photo demonstrates how your hand should look just after the notes have been plucked. The fingers should come up toward the palm of the hand, while the thumb moves away. If they collided instead, the angle of your picking hand was too extreme and should be adjusted.

Just after the notes have been plucked.

Arpeggios

To help to develop the good independence needed for fingerpicking, I've devoted this section to a group of longer pieces designed to work with many fingering combinations. The first one, simply an open-string arpeggio in E minor, helps you to become accustomed to this type of pattern.

We now see the same technique, only it's applied to moving chord changes, where the bass and lead notes shift strings.

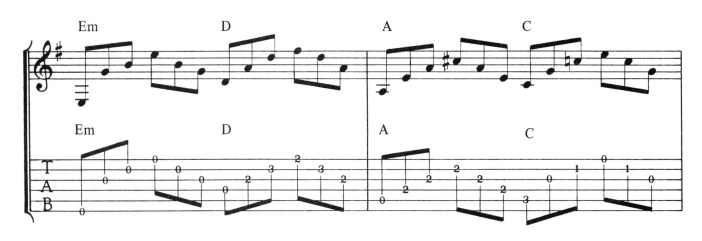

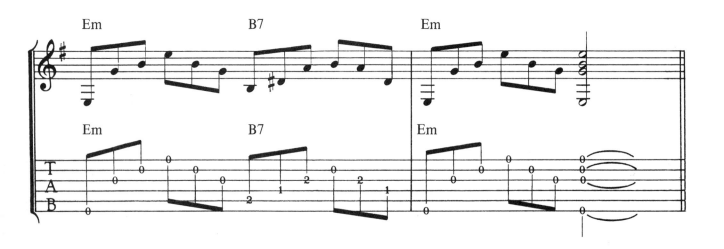

"Grabbing" the Chords

The act of "grabbing" a chord with four fingers is also one of the great advantages of fingerpicking. It's called "grabbed" because they are all played at once, and the proper position should feel as if your right hand is grabbing an object in its palm. In the following piece, you'll start to become used to this technique as it applies to shifting treble and bass notes.

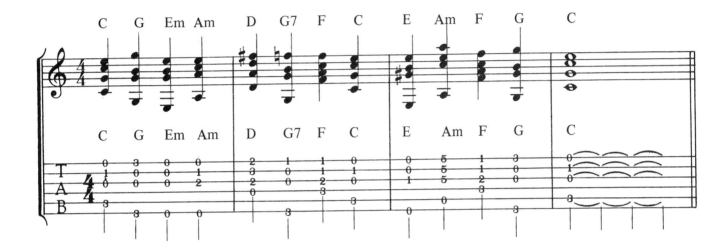

Learning to use broken, or irregular right-hand patterns is another difficult but rewarding part of the fingerpicking style. We see here how there are some notes that are played simultaneously with the bass notes, while others are independent.

Alternating Bass Notes

Patterns such as these are obviously based upon a strong rhythmic feeling, and until this rhythmic flow is achieved, they'll feel merely like groups of notes, rather than music. In the case of the next piece illustrating the complex usage of alternating bass notes, this attention to rhythm is especially crucial. Pay attention to just which notes are played with or without the bass notes, and the rhythmic concept will become much clearer to you. Practice it slowly at first, and build up speed as you get more into the "groove."

Alternating the bass notes gives the piece an even greater movement, and it helps to cover *all* six strings with the use of only four fingers. This technique will really come in handy in the Ragtime Guitar section later in this chapter. Note that some of the alternated bass notes are above the central *root* bass note, while others remain below it.

BLUES FINGERPICKING

This is certainly the earliest form of blues guitar playing, and once mastered, can be taken to great technical heights. Perhaps the most effective placement of this technique is when you have a lead line going on top and independent of the bass notes. This is one of the more challenging forms of fingerpicking, for it creates a sound of complete separation between the two parts. It is, and should be felt, as one continuous flowing part played by the right hand.

In this first "constant bass" exercise, we'll start by getting the thumb used to playing the constant bass in a shuffle feeling on the low E string. When you feel ready, and the thumb is working relatively independently, you should try to add some of the higher, lead notes. In this first piece we aren't going for a terribly wide spread between the bass and lead notes. We merely want to establish their relationship, while getting your picking hand used to playing both parts.

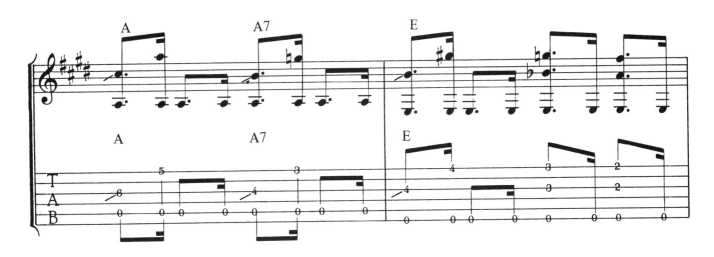

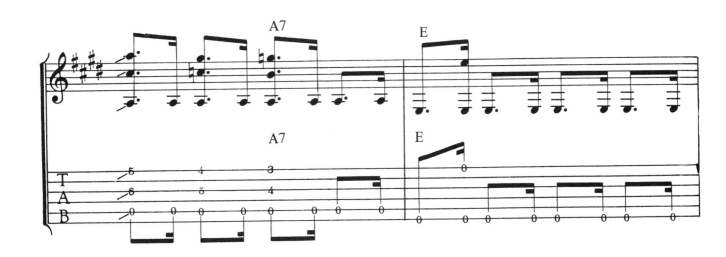

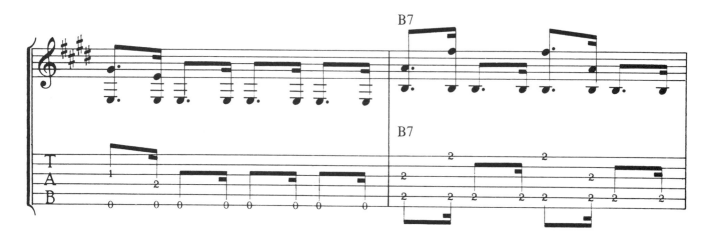

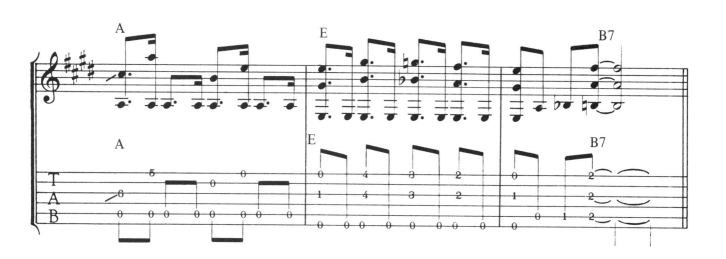

The Constant Bass

In this next constant bass piece we'll gain a further independence by adding special lead techniques, such as slides and hammer-ons. A good practice is to play two lead notes, while making the second hammered-on note land simultaneously with the picking of one of the bass note downbeats.

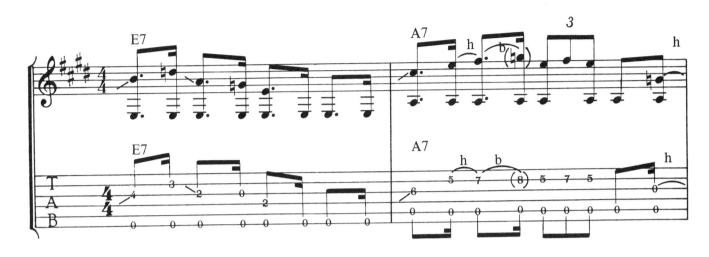

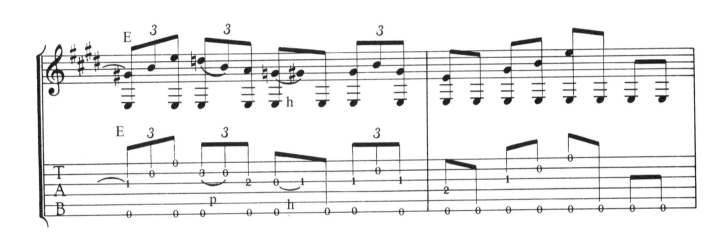

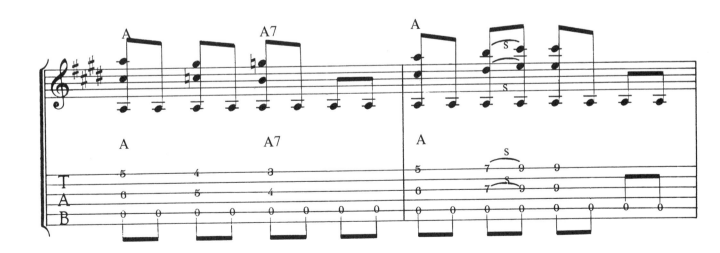

Triplets Over Eighth-Notes

Another great blues technique is to play triplets on the lead strings, while the bass part retains its shuffle feeling. This is easier than you'd think, because the shuffle is a triplet in disguise! The end result of all this is that you have three lead notes for every two bass notes. Quite obviously, this is a good technique to be applied to turnaround licks, due to the high incidence of triplets within turnarounds.

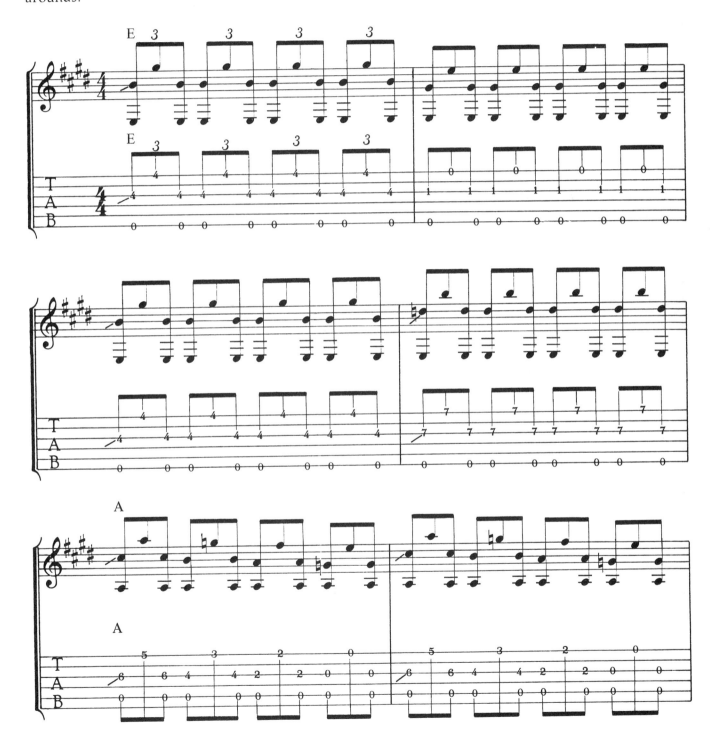

Fingerpicking with Lead Bends

Combining lead bends with the whole picture really brings the widest range of character to this blues technique. This demonstrates true control of the instrument, and therefore takes that much longer to master. I still want you to bend in the way I've been showing you, with the fingers helping to push the strings out of the way. This may seem inappropriate to you, but if played properly, the low E and A strings will remain clear of the top four strings, even during the bend. Obviously, this is essential to proper execution of this technique.

Right-Hand "Rolls"

This piece, one of my favorites for fingerpicking, is one of the most complex right-hand patterns I've ever attempted. What makes it so challenging is that it combines single-note lead and bass work with right-hand "rolls" and two-fingered picking strokes. This all requires an incredible amount of discipline and concentration to execute, particularly at a brisk tempo. I've chosen the key of D for this piece because both the open D and A chords lend themselves perfectly to the roll lick that is so key to this exercise. You'll note that only a *constant* bass is needed this time, as opposed to the shuffle eighth-note bass patterns of the previous exercises. Use an index-finger partial barre to create the D and A chords, because you'll need the extra fingers to play those notes on top of the roll patterns. Be sure to keep your fingerpicking consistent in its positioning, with the index, middle, and ring fingers coming up toward your palm, while the thumb moves away.

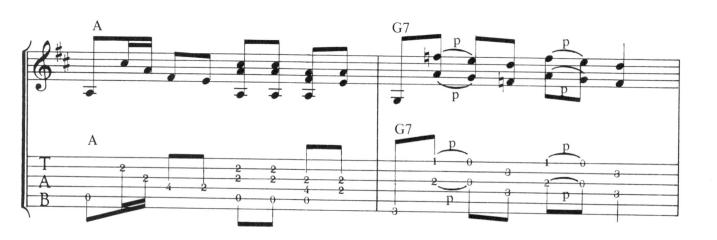

TRAVIS PICKING

The term *Travis* picking is coined from the greatest country fingerpicker who ever walked the face of the earth, none other than Merle Travis. This is an easy and well-supported statement to make, because his influence is so deeply felt on all levels of fingerpicking. Chet Atkins would be the first to acknowledge that his fingerpicking style owes everything to Travis. Roy Clark calls Merle his hero, and indeed, he'll forever be one of mine. A prolific and successful songwriter as well as a player and singer, Merle's most famous song was "Sixteen Tons," which was a giant hit for Tennessee Ernie Ford in the 1950s.

What made Merle's fingerpicking so unique was his ability to play completely separate and complex melodies on top of a chunky, rhythmic bass pattern. He further accentuated the bass–treble contrast by damping the low strings with the heel of his hand to create a thumpy bass tone that didn't sustain as long as the lead notes did. His influences were as much blues and ragtime as they were country, and his patterns were always fabulously danceable.

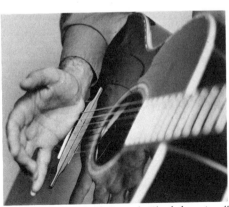

The position for Travis-style "heel-damping."

Merle Travis, 1976. (Credit: Bob Krueger)

This first little exercise shows the essence of the Travis picking style. To create the proper "thump" with the bass notes, you should damp the bottom three strings just after the bridge, as in this photo. Don't damp too high on the string, or you'll cut off all of the resonance.

Open and Closed Positions

Shifting positions is another factor of which to become aware in this type of playing, particularly when the use of open bass notes enables you to move the lead notes higher up the fingerboard. In this case, we see the same A7 Travis lick, in both open and closed forms.

In fact, this closed form of the A chord offers many melodic possibilities, and this piece shows only a few of the things I would experiment with if I were to improvise within this position.

Shifting Positions

The C7 chord form is a very useful one in Travis picking due to its extremely compact and movable design. Its use of the four middle strings keeps it transferable, and the high and low E strings, can be very conveniently damped out. In this photograph, we see how the C7 form should look when it's played up the neck. Note how I'm damping the two E strings.

D7 Chord in the C7 Form. Note thumb damping.

This chord form also lends itself nicely to alternating bass licks between the low A and E strings. In this exercise, we are playing this alternation as we continually move the chord form up the neck. Try to keep a nice, even rhythm with all of the fingerpicked notes.

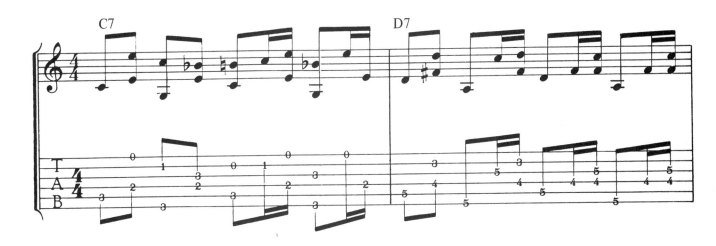

Travis Picking Solos

Each position on the guitar lends itself to so many different types of Travis picking that it is best illustrated with several solo pieces in the different locations. When you play in an open position like G, for example, and use some closed forms, such as E7, you must be aware of the differences and varying melodic capabilities within each position. In this first Travis picking exercise, we see the relative freedom that the open G position has over the closed D7. Also note that the G must alternate basses with the D string, while the D7 can use the lower E string for a similar purpose.

This is another open-position Travis piece, in open E, and this time we are combining even more chord forms, both open and closed. Try not to think faster than what your picking hand is capable of doing, particularly when it comes to tempo.

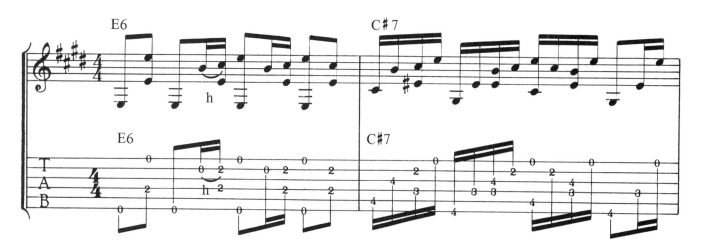

Perhaps we gain the most freedom for improvisation and octave splitting by using positions that involve closed chords *with* open strings in Travis picking. This piece, which ends with an interesting change of key, shows how we can use open strings that are *not* part of the chord as passing, melodic lead notes. This was one of Merle Travis' great

gifts, and I strongly suggest that you pick up whatever recordings you can find by him to help in your understanding of this unique and enjoyable style.

RAGTIME GUITAR

Ragtime music played on the guitar bears many similarities to Travis picking in that it uses the chord, bass, and melody approach as independent sounding parts. This is, of course, best characterized by the original ragtime instrument, the piano. In an attempt to imitate the archetypical left- and right-hand movement of the ragtime pianist, early ragtime players such as Blind Blake, Tampa Red, Big Bill Broonzy, Leadbelly, and Bo Carter developed some rather complex right-hand approaches to their soloistic music.

Very characteristic of this style was their use of alternating basses, double- and triple-note lead parts, and stop-time sections, where the bass part would disappear. This allowed the artist to play a single-note

Blind Blake. (Courtesy Biograph Records, Inc.)

fill that would showcase some of his fancier lead work and showmanship. These fills would often come between vocal lines, "answering" the words in an almost "question-and-answer" manner. Blind Blake was perhaps the finest exponent of this technique, and was quite respected in his day for his virtuosity.

"Diddy Wa Diddy"

The following is my own arrangement of one of Blake's true classics, "Diddy Wa Diddy," a song that beautifully illustrates his syncopated, ragtimey style.

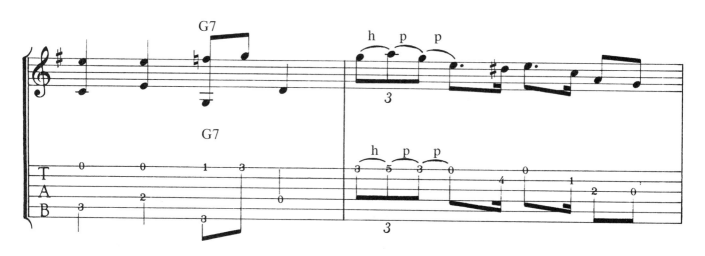

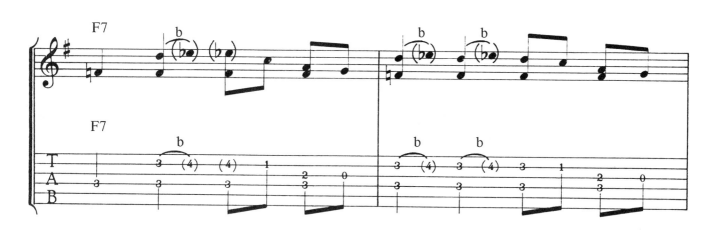

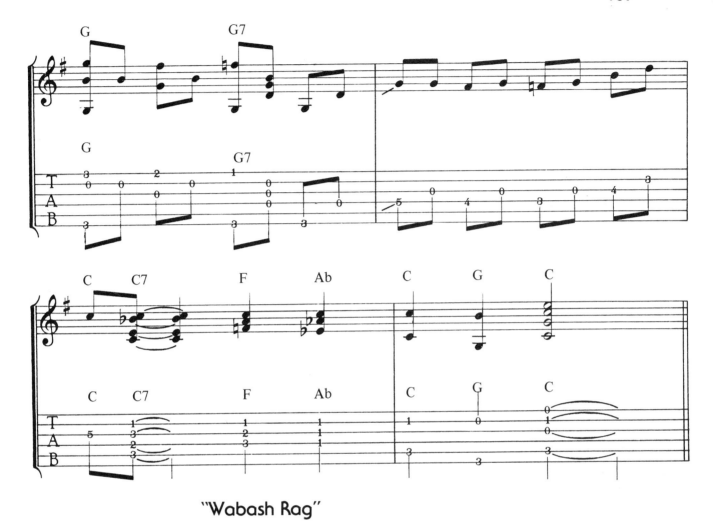

"Wabash Rag"

The "Wabash Rag" is also one of the true ragtime classics, and illustrates ragtime's occasional use of odd-time measures and unusual, circular chord changes. This is similar to what most players refer to as the famous "Salty Dog" chord progression.

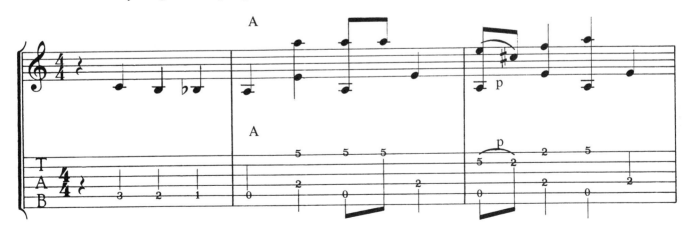

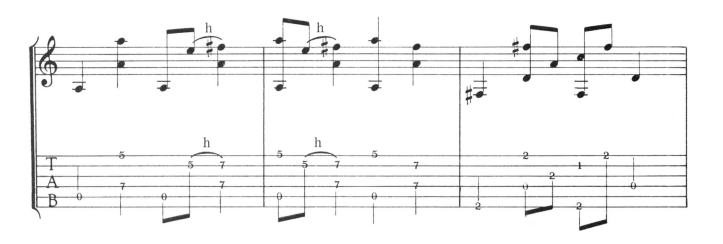

SLIDE GUITAR

Slide, or bottleneck guitar as many like to call it, is primarily a blues style that originated in the Mississippi Delta area of the deep South, probably around the time of the early 1920s. At that particular time, traveling minstrel shows were very popular in the rural areas, and many of these shows featured "exotic" Hawaiian musicians and performers. Hawaiian guitar is played in a horizontal slide position and the notes are created by a bar placed over the strings. It is believed that around this time, aspiring guitarists from the South saw this and began to mimic the whining, almost vocal sound of the Hawaiian players. They would tune their guitars to open chords and use either a knife, bone, bottleneck, or any similar resonant, smooth object to slide along the strings. These new bottleneck guitarists would play in the standard upright position, and unlike the Hawaiian style players, would combine fretted single-note and chord work *with* the slide playing. This technique soon proved to be of great emotional value to blues music, and guitarists such as Robert Johnson, Son House, Bukka White, and Charley Patton brought attention to this new art form through their

Bukka White.

recordings and shows. In the 1940s and 1950s, this musical tradition traveled to the northern cities, most notably Chicago, whose South Side has nurtured a long and vital blues tradition. Chicago players took on a more urban, "uptown" sound, donning electric guitars and often performing with full bands. This Chicago blues slide sound was best exemplified by the playing of such greats as Elmore James, Muddy Waters, and Tampa Red, and its influence is still heard in the sound of today's biggest rock acts. At times, the Rolling Stones sound like no more than an English, white version of a late 1950s South Side blues band, or a rural acoustic blues duo.

Muddy Waters.

Anyone who desires to be a complete acoustic guitarist today is well aware of the importance of the slide guitar in a player's vocabulary. Modern slide artists like Ry Cooder and Johnny Winter, and the late greats Duane Allman and Lowell George, have kept its popularity alive, while new audiences are introduced to slide guitar every day. It is truly one aspect of electric and acoustic blues that will never die!

Setting the Guitar Up for Slide Playing

The fact that we are now using an object to create notes with our left hand rather than actually fretting the notes has certain prerequisites. When playing slide, one doesn't want the string to actually touch the fingerboard from the slide's pressure. Therefore, it is important that the "action," or height of the strings, be just high enough to facilitate both slide playing and normal fretting should you so desire. One must also take into account that open tunings, favored in slide playing, increase string tension, and this also helps to maintain the string's resistance to the slide itself.

You should try to use the heaviest string possible for slide playing, again to help in sustain and resistance to the weight of the slide. However, I have found that you can use regular acoustic light gauge for all general applications, and that the bronze-wound variety offers the best slide tone.

The Slide

Through the decades, countless objects have been used as slides by guitarists. A few of the choices are pictured here, and no doubt there are countless others. (A beer bottle or a microphone stand has worked wonders for me in a pinch.) I still find that after all the experimentation is done, something with good weight and resonance works best for me. For this reason, I generally prefer the brass variety that is relatively heavy and can be found in many of the better music stores today. Beware of the thin, dull-sounding objects that are also sold in many of these music stores as slides. They just won't cut the mustard. When trying out the slide, please make sure that the slide allows your pinky to show through just enough so that the finger can sense the notes that are being reached. You must also beware of putting on a slide that seems just a little too snug; I can only too clearly remember the *hour* I spent in a New York music shop desperately trying to get a glass slide off my poor little finger!

As far as sound is concerned, you'll find that glass will produce a more transparent, eerie sound on the acoustic guitar, while the brass or metal slides will produce a fatter, brighter tone. Glass also tends to have many imperfections and inconsistencies and can cause certain "dropouts" in the sustain of the notes. Be sure to try out both before you decide what's right for you.

Assortment of slides.

Holding the Slide

The photo we have here illustrates the generally proper position for holding the slide. You'll note that I prefer having it on my pinky, which frees three fingers in a row for fretting and chord work. You'll also see that I advocate laying the other three fingers on top of the strings behind the slide to help damp out any overtones that might occur. The slide should also always remain perpendicular to the strings, and directly *over* the fret. Avoid tilting the slide unnecessarily. This will create inconsistency in pitch, something that is far too common among slide guitarists.

Proper slide position.

The Right Hand in Slide Playing

Fingerpicking, while an optional technique for most guitarists, is, I feel, a true necessity for the slide player. The main reason lies in the incredible damping capabilities that it affords you, as well as the overall better control you have over the destiny of the notes! This is so important in a style of playing that uses such a non-discriminating object as a slide. You'll find that if you play a scale with the slide, and *don't* damp, your notes will end up in a complete *blur,* with no resultant subtlety.

To illustrate simply what I mean by all this damping talk, here are two very easy exercises. In this initial one, you see that if the lick moves toward the *low* E string, the very same fingers that plucked the strings now serve to dampen them when you no longer want them to ring. The photo shows the position of the hand at the very end of the lick, after the damping has occurred.

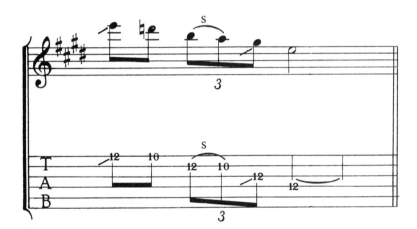

Position after notes have been damped out while moving toward the low E string.

In this lick, moving toward the *high* E string, we see that in order to let only the last note ring, we must use our thumb, coming across and stopping both the G and B strings simultaneously.

Well, now that we've covered much of the physical side of slide playing, let's make some music!

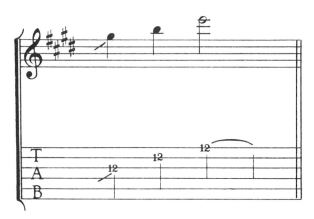

The thumb damps as the lick moves toward the high E string.

Slide Guitar in Standard Tuning

Although it is not a traditional technique and is a style of slide playing that probably limits the player more than anything, this approach has caught on in recent years. This is particularly the case when a player wants to alternate between slide and standard lead work to add some depth and flash to his or her playing. The main difference between standard tuning slide and using open tunings is that here we must cover wider areas of the fingerboard in order to obtain the right patterns. The ability to play chords and harmony note work is also greatly diminished, but by no means eliminated.

The Standard Tuning Blues Pattern

There is one pattern in particular that I always use if called on to play standard tuning slide. This is a relatively long scale, and although it does traverse quite a bit of the neck, it does contain one very useful "box" pattern. This box, or group of closely related notes, exists in the middle of the scale, and is based upon the A-chord format. Diagram 9 shows the standard tuning pattern for the key of E, with brackets around the box position.

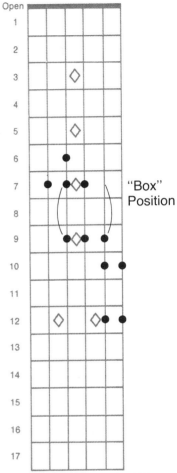

Diagram 9. Standard Tuning Pattern for E

Standard Tuning Slide Licks

The following are a group of my favorite licks from this position. Keep the damping technique in mind, both toward you, and away from you; and remember to maintain the three-finger approach even when leaving the top three strings to continue the lick. Take all of these riffs slowly at first, so all the nuances have a better chance to develop within your playing.

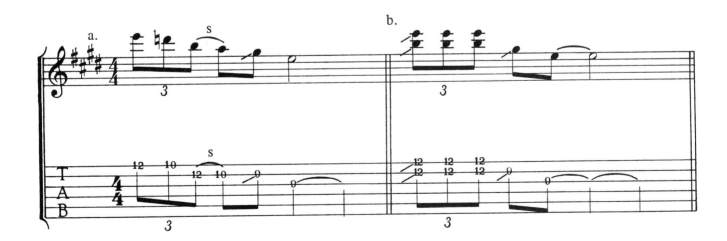

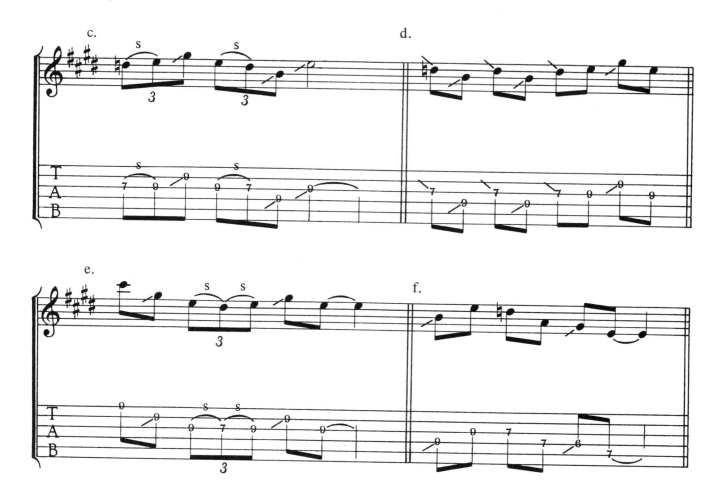

Open Tunings For Slide Guitar

Open tunings are a very useful tool for the guitarist in general, and entirely new musical possibilities exist within these altered formats. Of course, for slide they're almost a necessity, and make the use of an object such as a bottleneck much more feasible. These open tunings were developed in the early days of rural blues guitar, and indeed, open tuning experiments are always going on wherever inventive guitarists can be found. The two most common tuning configurations are open E and G. The former is often tuned down a whole step to D, and the latter can at times be brought up to open A. This is, of course, if your guitar can take the strain! You can raise the tuning and the keys by using a capo, but beware of the strings getting too close to the frets to have a clean slide sound. With the use of open tunings we now have an open chord always at our disposal, and the harmonic possibilities become quite different than what we've grown accustomed to in standard tuning. In this section, we'll be looking at the two most popular tunings, with their similarities and differences.

SLIDE GUITAR IN OPEN E TUNING

This is probably the most widely used open tuning of them all, and is particularly evident in the hard-driving styles of Elmore James, Tampa Red, Duane Allman, and Johnny Winter, to name a few. It's been my personal favorite for years, and I feel that the possibilities available to the lead player within this tuning far outnumber the other tunings.

In the Diagram 10 chord charts, we can see some of the new chord positions that arise from the altered pitches of the strings. You'll note that the G string now gets raised to a G♯, the D string is tuned up to an E, and the A string is also raised up a whole step to a B. We now actually have three E notes, all of different octaves within one open chord.

In Diagram 11 we see the chords that can be created in E tuning at the different frets either by barreing or with the use of the slide.

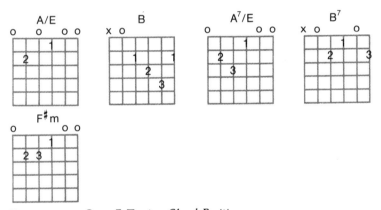

Diagram 10. Open E Tuning Chord Positions

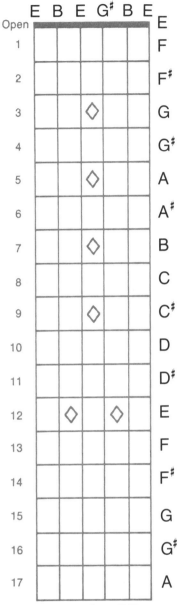

Diagram 11. Open E Tuning—
Barre Chords

The Open E Tuning "Box" Pattern

Through my own playing I have found that two basic blues scales are the most economic and accessible for playing blues and rock licks in open E tuning. The first scale begins at the twelfth fret (for the key of E), and I call it a "box" pattern (Diagram 12) because it involves notes that, for the most part, span only two or three frets. Here it is in notation and in diagram form, and when practicing it, please try to use the slides between notes as I've indicated for you.

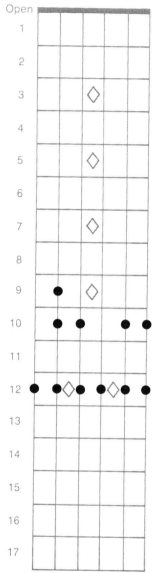

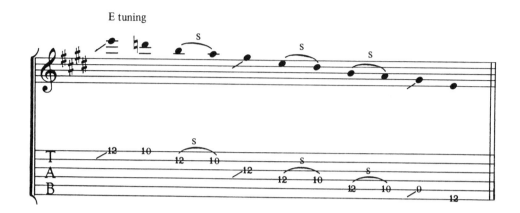

Diagram 12. Open E Tuning—
Box Pattern

The Open Position Scale

The other blues scale I like to use for slide is the open position blues scale for E tuning (Diagram 13). It contains quite a few open-string notes, hence its name. The notes and dots in parentheses are closed substitutions for their open-stringed counterparts.

Licks in Open E Tuning

There are countless possibilities available to the lead player in open E tuning, in both the open and "box" positions. Although they are quite extensive, the group of licks I've chosen here only scratch the creative surface. I do hope, however, that they inspire you to go on and create some new ones of your own. Remember to maintain the proper damping techniques we already discussed, and you'll be well on your way toward creating the proper sound. Keep those fingers moving in groups of three, all the way toward the low E string when playing these licks. Also, make sure to damp out the notes only at the *precise* moment the next note is sounded. This will definitely smooth out the sound, and will avoid the staccato effect that "overdamping" can bring.

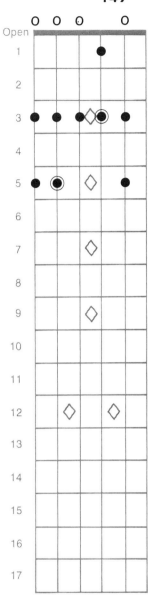

Diagram 13. Open Position Blues Scale—E Tuning

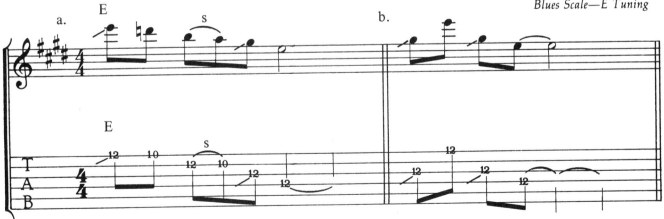

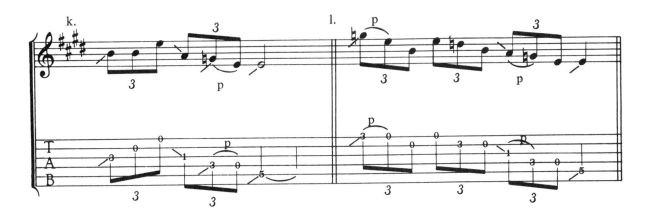

Open E Tuning Slide Piece

In the 12-bar blues that follows, the lead licks and phrases I've chosen are developed from the two scale positions with which we've been working. Take note of the subtleties in phrasing, and in the implications of the chord changes within the runs themselves. In fact, when you try some improvising on your own, be sure to attempt to "hear" the chord change within the single-note passages you're playing. Use sevenths when going from the I chord to the IV, major thirds on the I, and minor thirds (sevenths) on the IV, and the other melodic flavorings that can convey chord structure and movement.

152

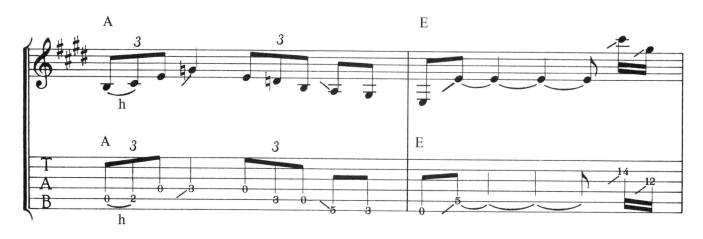

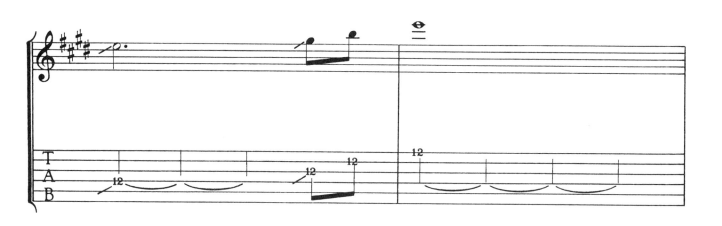

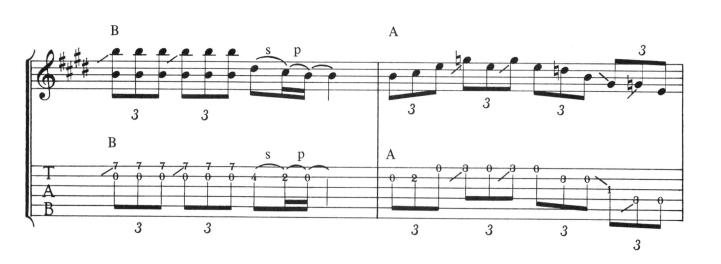

The "Dust My Broom" Lick

No study on slide guitar would be complete without this blues classic created by probably the most influential slide player in history, the great Elmore James. One of the most important and powerful bluesmen of the golden era of the South Side, his music was a direct link between the rural Mississippi blues of Robert Johnson and the electric urban blues of Chicago. He was one of the very first to play slide on an amplified guitar, in fact much of his work was performed on an acoustic instrument with a pickup mounted in the soundhole. His urgent, incredibly intense sound influenced an entire new generation of black and white players, and a keen ear can hear a little Elmore in almost anyone who's playing slide guitar. His recording of Robert Johnson's acoustic classic "Dust My Broom," was, for a blues record, an enormous hit, and his slide lick used on the "hook" of the tune has become the most imitated in all of blues history. So popular was James' version of this song that his band was almost always called "The Broomdusters."

Here is both the legendary "hook" line, as well as the more verse-like solo with which he frequently liked to follow up. Don't be afraid to play this one with a lot of stinging intensity, for this is the way it's always sounded best, especially in Elmore James' hands!

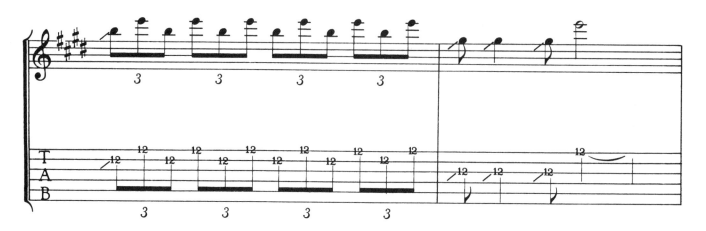

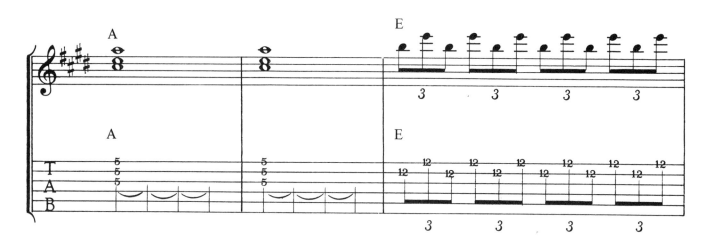

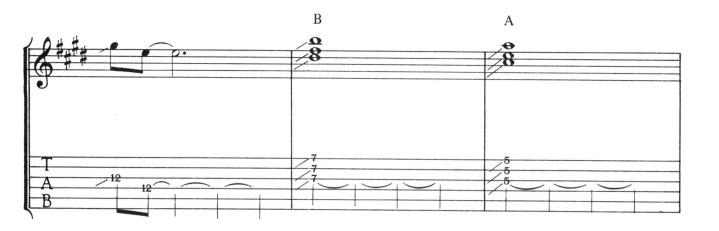

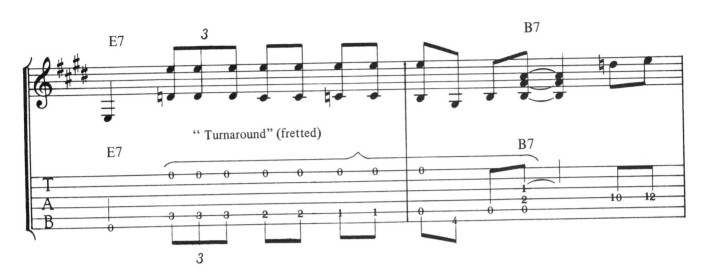

" Turnaround" (fretted)

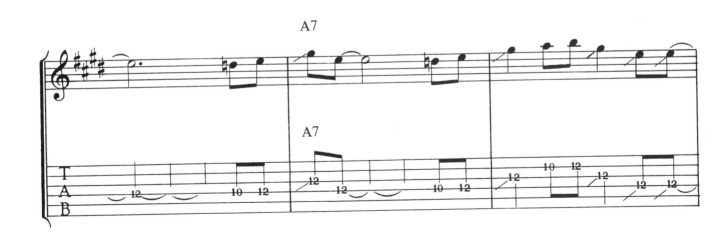

SLIDE GUITAR IN OPEN G TUNING

Open G or A tuning is more closely related to the traditional acoustic blues styles, and is exemplified by the work of bluesmen like Robert Johnson, Skip James, Charley Patton, and Son House, all from the Mississippi Delta region. An attractive quality of this tuning is its rather high, almost banjo-like timbre. This would become even more apparent if you were to take it up a whole step to open A, but please don't attempt this unless you're sure that your neck and strings can take it! Another special feature of this tuning is that you now have two octaves of D as well as two octaves of G. This opens up many more interesting fingerpicking possibilities, and with the addition of that nice, fat low D note, the V chord can have a fuller sound than in the E tuning position. We also now have a greater chance to make use of alternating bass note work due to the two octaves that are available for both G and D.

Blues Scales in Open G Tuning: Open and Closed Positions

There are two extremely useful scales for improvising in this tuning, and just like their E tuning counterparts, they take the form of both open and closed box positions. You'll take special note that the highest root note, very important to the blues, now exists on the fifth fret of the high E string, instead of being the highest open string, as in E tuning.

Here is the closed position for G tuning, and as you can see, it does cover a bit more distance on the neck than the closed E tuning box pattern.

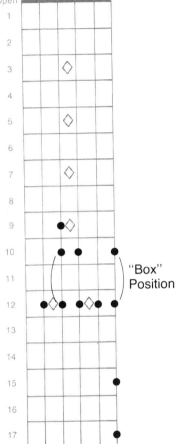

Diagram 14. *G Tuning—Closed "Box" Position*

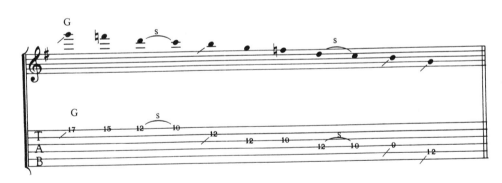

The open blues scale position for G tuning (Diagram 15) does relate quite closely to the note relationships found in the open E scale, and as we can see, the notes are all moved up one string, and the high root exists on the fifth fret of the E string.

158

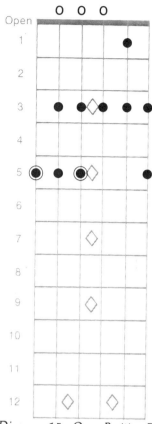

Diagram 15. Open Position Blues Scale—G Tuning

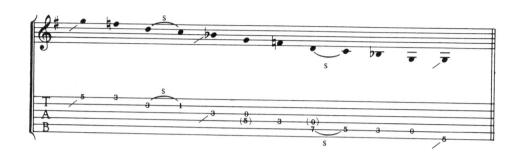

Licks In Open G Tuning

This selection makes quite a broad use of open G tuning, and although they readily relate to the E tuning licks, differences also exist. This, again, is particularly apparent when reaching your high root notes, as well as the other key slide positions.

G Tuning Solo Exercise

This piece, also a 12-bar blues, is even deeper in the country blues tradition than our E tuning work, and is very reminiscent of the early acoustic work of the Delta blues artists. Try to take notice of its relationships to the open E positions, and please try not to confuse the two; for this is a common occurrence when learning new scale positions. After a while, when your confidence grows, I hope you spend some time trying some of your own creative ideas within this tuning. Good luck with it!

160

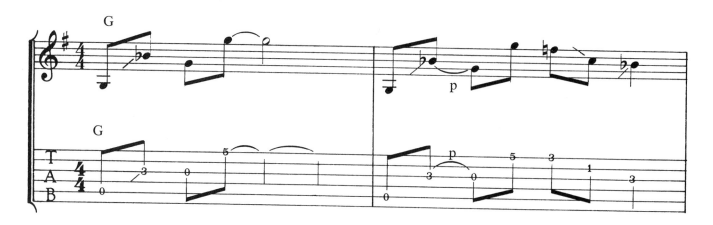

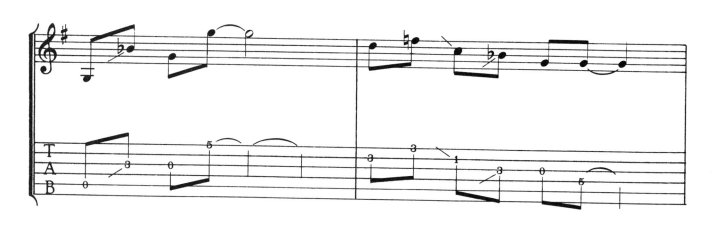

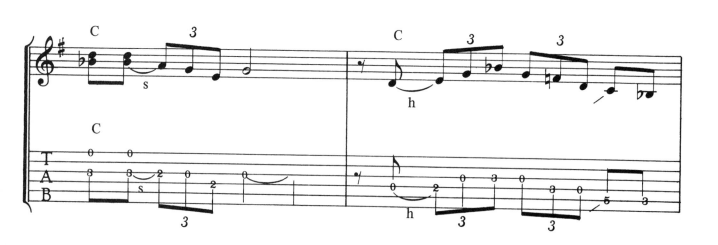

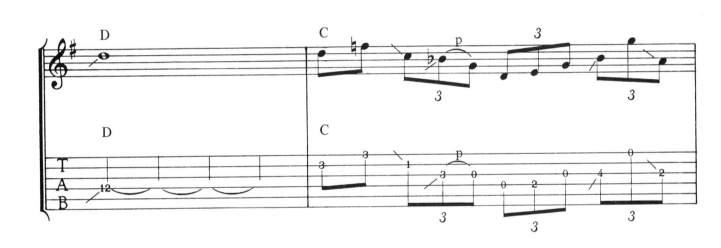

5

LEAD ACOUSTIC ROCK GUITAR

Although it is usually thought of as an electric guitar's domain, rock music should certainly not be kept out of an acoustic guitarist's vocabulary. Firmly based in a blues background, much of the rock sound is owed to the innovators such as Chuck Berry, Robert Johnson, B. B. King, etc., and if you wanted to, you could actually draw a "family tree" of guitarists that leads from the Delta Blues styles right up to Heavy Metal!

Of course, acoustic guitar has always held a firm place in the rock sound, but this has always been in the accompanimental form of rhythm parts and has rarely taken the lead role. In this section, to help you better grasp the rock styles, we'll be taking what are essentially electric guitar approaches and applying them to the acoustic instrument. As I mentioned in the Chapter 3 on Blues Styles, the acoustic guitar *does* limit you in terms of the extent with which you can use string bending, and of course, is slightly more difficult to play than most electric guitars; therefore, some changes in approach will be rather evident.

One great lesson that rock playing on an acoustic instrument can teach us is that while electric guitars rely greatly on their amplified volume and sustain, acoustic guitars must be worked harder to create a similarly powerful effect. We can't, of course, expect the same results all the time, but we *do* end up creating an interesting blend of both styles that can lead, I hope, to your *own* style!

THE "PARTIAL BARRE"
IN ROCK PLAYING

Because the majority of the scales that are the basis of rock playing have already been covered in the Blues and Country chapters, this section will introduce some new and different applications for these scales.

The "partial barre" is something upon which both rock lead *and* rhythm guitarists rely quite heavily. Artists like Jimi Hendrix, Jimmy Page, Eric Clapton, and countless other influential guitarists have used this technique to help develop the expressiveness of their instrument. In simple terms, the "partial barre" is the barreing of any number of strings less than the full six, and is used to help create positions where new licks can be developed. This is mainly due to the fact that the barres enable the guitarist to create patterns that are not possible by using only standard single-string work.

This "partial barre" scale is a very useful rock pattern that is reminiscent of the work of the great Jimi Hendrix and Eric Clapton. By using the barre in key locations, we're bridging some important positions within the rock scale, thereby creating new and interesting possibilities. Make sure to use your first finger for each of the barres.

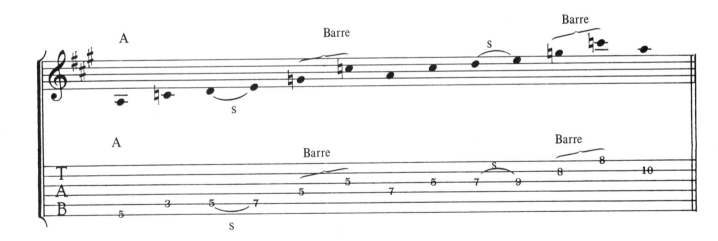

These two barre positions, one octave apart, have given birth to some of rock's most memorable licks. When playing the runs that follow, make sure to use the barres *only* when they're necessary for the execution of the notes, rather than holding them down indefinitely, putting unecessary strain on your left hand.

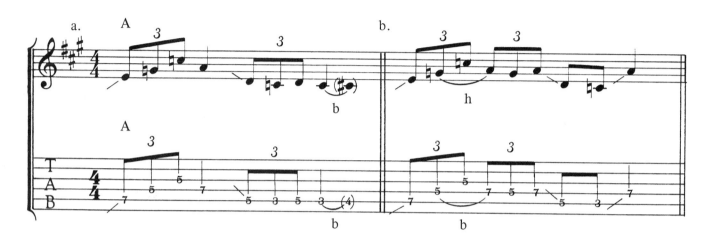

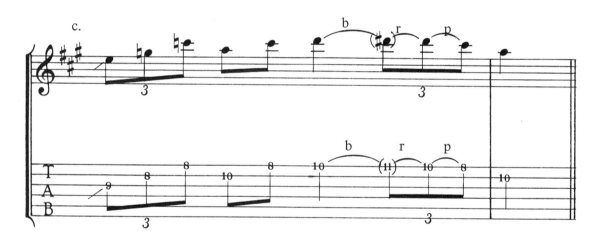

Rapid-Fire Pull-Off Licks

Partial barres also enable you to create the many "flash" style licks often heard in the playing of influentials such as Jimmy Page, Billy Gibbons, and Eddie Van Halen. These "rapid-fire" pull-offs, as I like to call them, help create the illusion of extremely fast playing by the use of partial barres, usually on the top two strings. When playing the exercises that follow, please keep in mind that the pull-off is really a *left-hand pluck* that gives new life and sustain to the string.

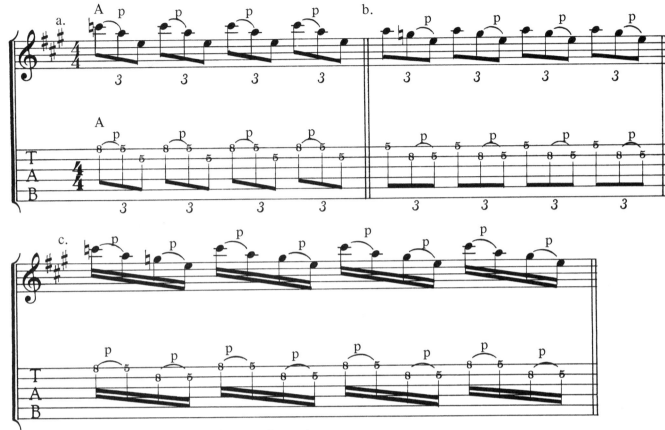

Adding String Bending

Adding the technique of string bending to these licks can really make you sound like a masterful rock player. It's also a way to further develop the skill of bending cleanly and accurately to the right pitch. This is because most of the licks play the *fretted* version of the note just before the bent version of that *same* note is played. This gives your ear the proper note to aim for in the bending process. The following licks combine these techniques. Remember to commit your *entire* hand to the bends.

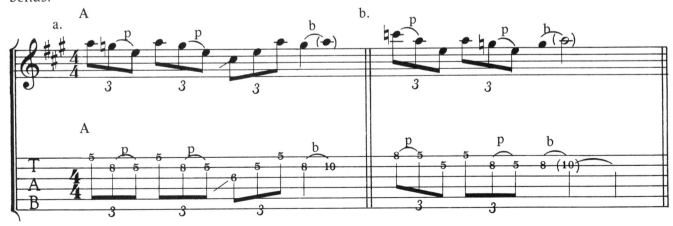

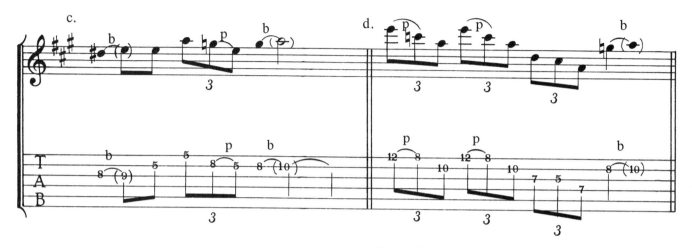

Adding Hammer-ons

If we now add the technique of hammering-on to the rock arsenal, we see that almost no means of expression is beyond our grasp. By adding hammer-ons, we're able to create what I call "roll" licks, that have a decidedly smooth, yet fast style. You'll note that many of these use a *three*-note barre covering the top three strings, rather than the two-note barres with which we've been working thus far.

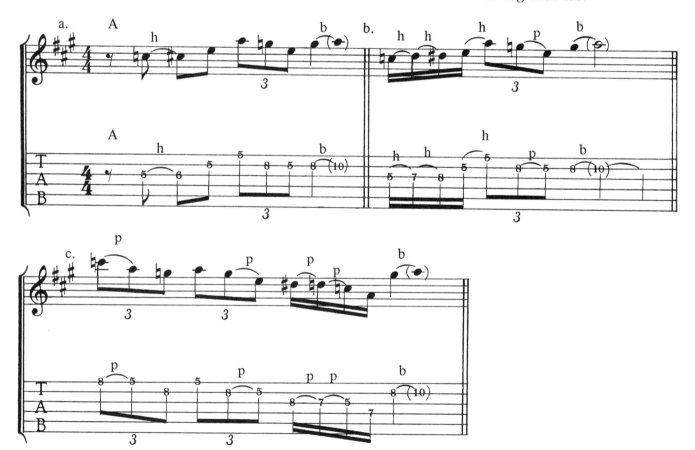

CHROMATIC STYLE ROCK PLAYING

As far as fast playing is concerned, there is no technique quite as impressive as being able to pick *each* note. This comes more easily to some than others, but is a welcome addition to anyone's technical prowess. In fact, hammer-ons and pull-offs only simulate what a true rapid picker can accomplish. Anyone who's ever seen or heard players such as Steve Morse, Larry Coryell, John McLaughlin, or Al DiMeola knows the technical virtuosity to which I'm referring, and is surely aware of the hard work and dedication it takes to master this style.

Steve Morse. (Credit: Arlen Roth)

One of the key elements in being able to *find* places for this technique on the fingerboard is locating positions for *chromatic* runs. These are runs that go from one fret to the next, either up or down, without skipping frets. To illustrate what I mean, and to help you to develop this technique, I've written out an open-position chromatic scale that uses all six strings. Try playing it with even up-and-down picking strokes.

Many scales can also be turned into chromatic runs, such as the blues scale that follows. Here, we use our first, second, and third fingers to walk up in groups of three for each element of the scale. In this manner, we're actually able to create nine notes out of what once was a three-note segment of the scale.

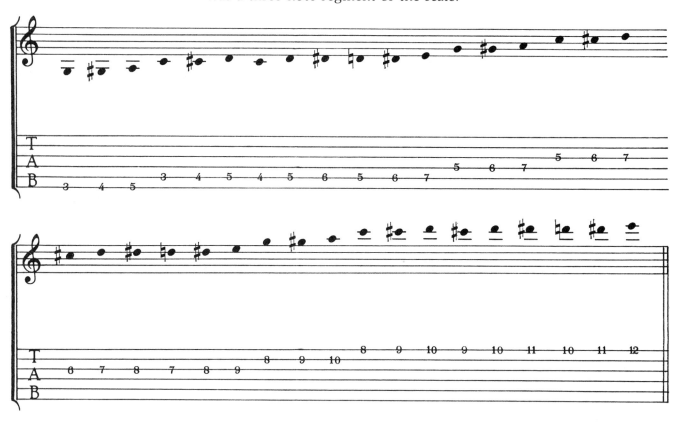

The rock runs that follow show just some of the very fast licks that can be played using the chromatic style. Make sure to pick every note, and if you find it too difficult to do it quickly, slow it down so you can build up your technique before you can build up your speed. Enjoy them!

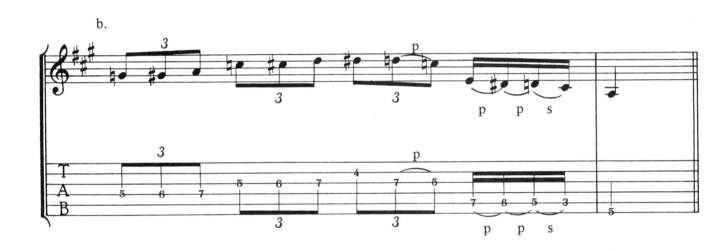

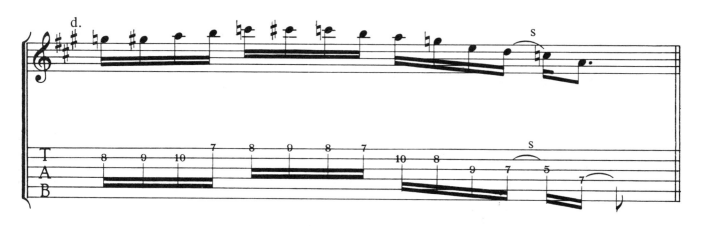

ROCK SOLOING

Soloing is when we put it all together and really express ourselves, and sadly, many guitarists can play lots of fast notes, but have trouble completing the kinds of musical thoughts needed in soloing. I hope this little section can begin to head off this problem for you, and help you better understand the art of soloing.

What the content of a solo is, of course, is dictated by first, the melody of the tune; second, the chord changes; and third, the improvisational ability and expressiveness of the player. In rock soloing, there is a powerful blend of chord awareness and technical "flash," while at the same time, one should be aware of melodic strengths. These are the elements that you should listen for when studying solos by the greats, while paying particularly close attention to the artist's thought patterns as they translate onto the fingerboard.

Having already touched upon soloing over I–IV–V changes in the Blues chapter (Chapter 3), we can now go on to some more challenging rock chord progressions and ideas. One of the most often used progressions in rock since the late 1960s has been the I–VII–IV change. More prevalent than ever before, this type of progression has become a real favorite of heavy metal bands, and is often the basis for some extremely powerful, emotional soloing. In the exercise that I've written out for the changes E–D–A, you'll see how the juxtaposition of the E blues/rock scale over the D chord creates a very pleasing tension. This is then partially resolved by going to the A, or IV chord, which uses the flatted thirds, and then finally comes back "home" to the E chord. Please make use of all the bends, hammer-ons, etc. that I've indicated to get the most intensity out of this rock solo.

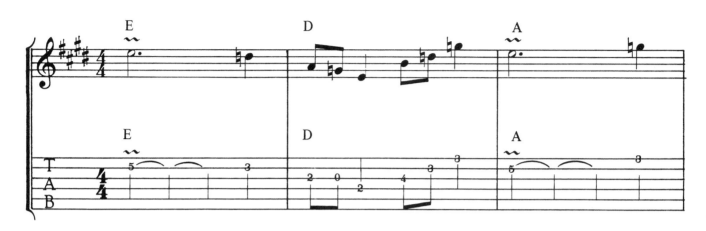

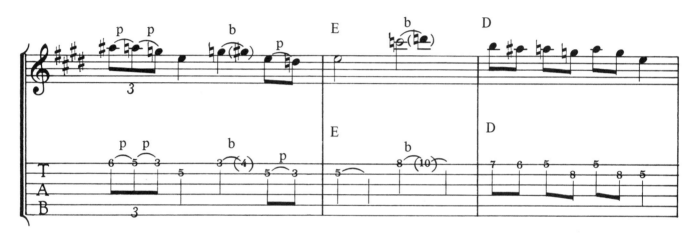

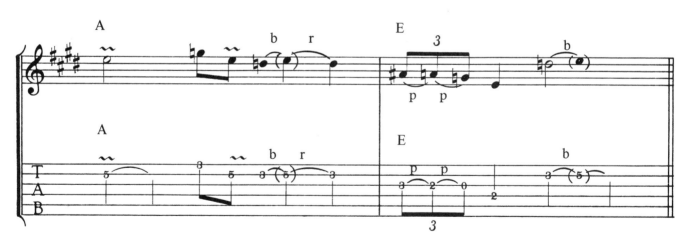

This progression E–B–C♯ minor–D–A is another popular "power" chord change often heard in heavy metal music, and represents a bit more of harmonic challenge than the previous exercise. Note that while we tend to stay around the same single-note positions, the notes themselves are paying more attention to the chord changes themselves, allowing the chords to dictate the melodic content of the solo.

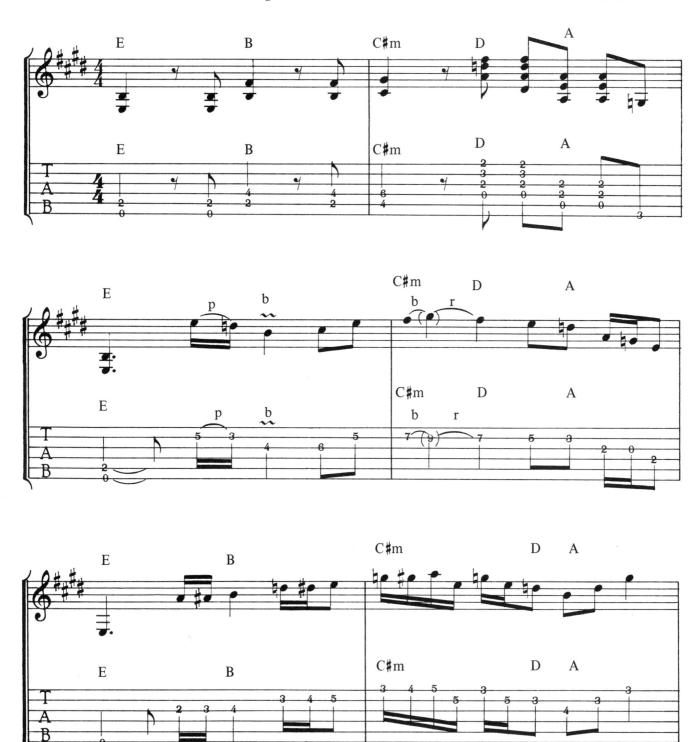

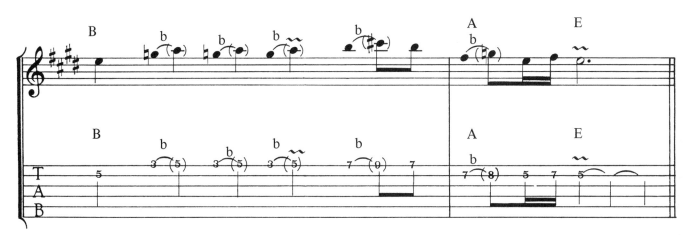

This final exercise uses a powerful I–V–VI minor–IV change for the key of G, and represents the kind of chord progression heard often in country rock as well as hard rock. Due to the structure of the song, especially the use of a root and its relative minor, I've chosen to work mostly with the major pentatonic scale for G. Going back to our country section will tell us how we make this the *minor* pentatonic scale for E minor, while never shifting positions. As you'll see in this, our final rock solo, it's which notes we accent harmonically that best convey the chord change to the listener, a good rule to always keep in mind!

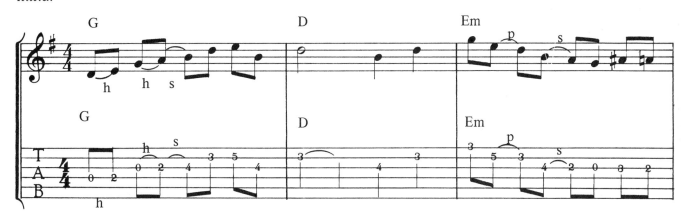

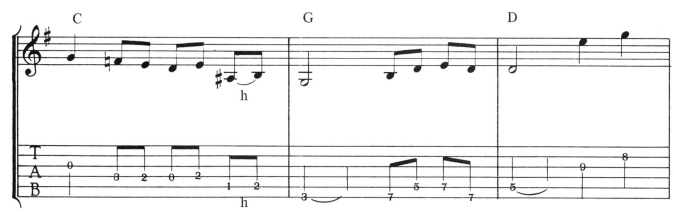

174

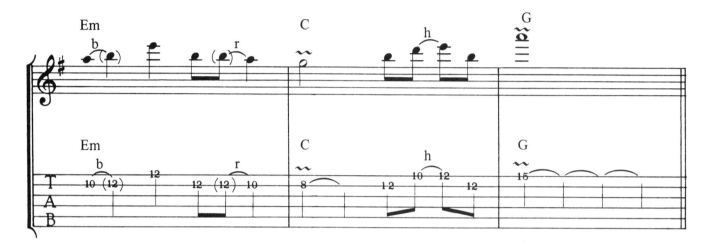

JAZZ STYLES

Jazz guitar has been enjoying a much wider acceptance among acoustic musicians these days, and indeed, has come the full cycle since it began on acoustic instruments a long time ago. Masters of acoustic jazz such as Larry Coryell, John McLaughlin, and Al DiMeola have taken this musical form to many new places and have certainly helped spawn a new generation of harmonically and technically sophisticated players.

Jazz is a music of improvisation. Even its chord theory reflects an experimental form of *substitution* based upon the more standard changes and positions. This chord substitution approach is one of the basic techniques an aspiring jazz guitarist should acquire. Before we go on with the studies of these various progressions, let's first look at Diagram 16 for some of the new chord positions of which we should be aware in jazz guitar.

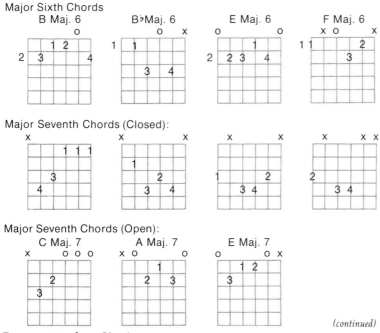

Diagram 16. Jazz Chords

(continued)

Diagram 16. Jazz Chords (cont.)

Maj. 7 & 9 (Closed):

E Maj. 7 & 9 (Open):

Maj. 6 & 9 (Closed):

B♭ 6 & 9 (Open):

F 6 & 9 (Open):

Minor Sixth Chords (Closed):

  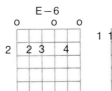

Minor Sixth Chords (Open):

B−6

B♭−6

E−6

F−6

A−6

Minor Seventh Chords (Closed):

(Open:) B−7

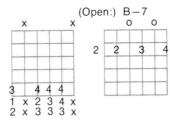

A−7

E−7

Minor 11 (Closed):

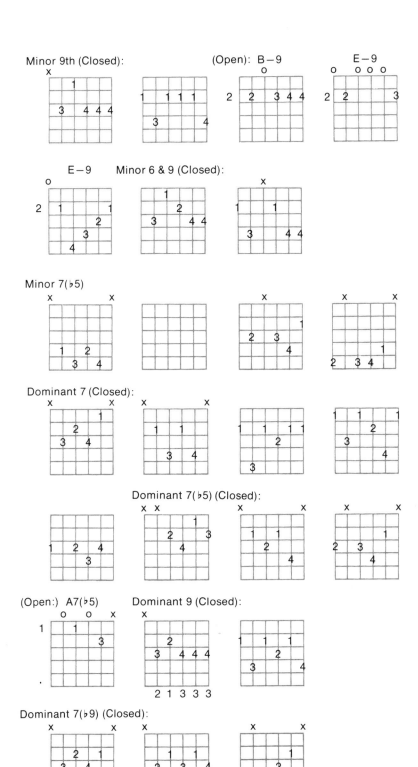

Minor 9th (Closed):

(Open): B–9

E–9

E–9

Minor 6 & 9 (Closed):

Minor 7(♭5)

Dominant 7 (Closed):

Dominant 7(♭5) (Closed):

(Open:) A7(♭5)

Dominant 9 (Closed):

Dominant 7(♭9) (Closed):

(continued)

Diagram 16. Jazz Chords (cont.)

Dominant 7(♯9) (Closed):

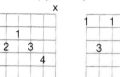

Dominant 13

Dominant 13 (Cont.):

Dom. 7(♭13)

Dom. 9(♭5)

Augmented Chords
(Closed):

(Open): E+

A+   D+

Diminished Chords (Closed):

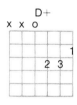

(Open:) F°   B♭°

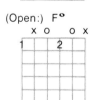

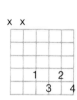

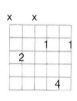

D°

CHORD SUBSTITUTION

We can begin to understand jazz chord substitution by transforming the standard I–IV–V blues progression into a more complex, musically interesting format. By using such new jazz chord forms as major sevenths and augmented chords, we see how they can become "passing" chords that help the overall movement of the piece.

This first chord exercise makes use of the traditional "comping" style so prevalent in the big band and swing days. Note also that we are using a very "closed" form of C7 to keep all of the chords within a close harmonic proximity of each other. This is a good practice to use when playing jazz chord progressions because it keeps the fingerings close and enables you to "voice" the chords within relatively close "boxes."

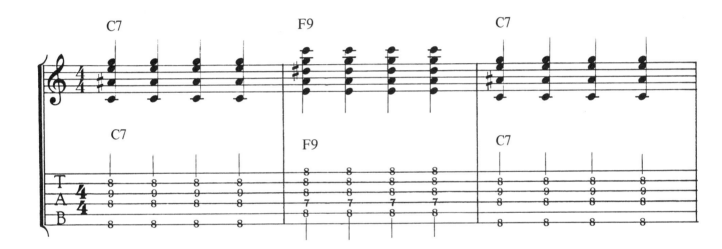

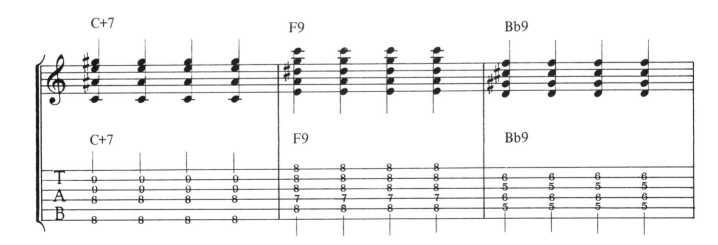

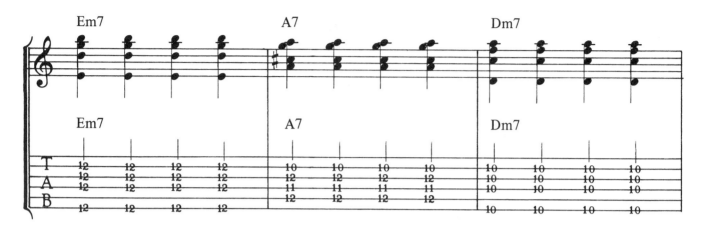

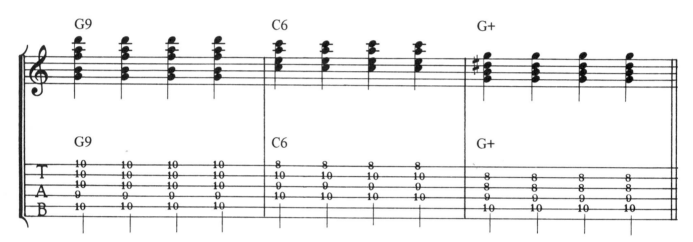

Turnarounds

In this jazz piece, we see how "closed" position chords can be "walked" to create a nice, moving turnaround. Note that the chords are walking in very much the same way you would hear a "walking" bass line in jazz.

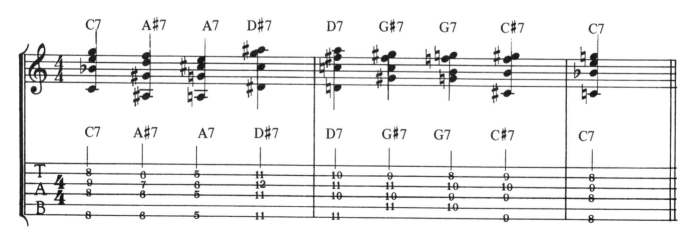

Jazz Arpeggios

Perhaps the first and easiest way to begin jazz improvisation is by using arpeggios. In this manner, we're able to "see" these new and unusual chords on the fingerboard, and rather than dealing with new scales, we simply "break up" the chords into these melodic patterns. Here, for example, is a very commonly used but effective arpeggio lick for a position of a major seventh chord.

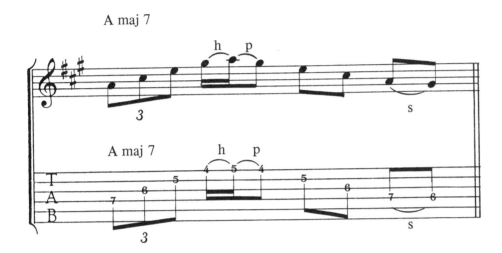

The augmented chord also has a position that lends itself readily to arpeggiation. This particular lick resolves to the I, or tonic chord, treating the augmented as a fifth.

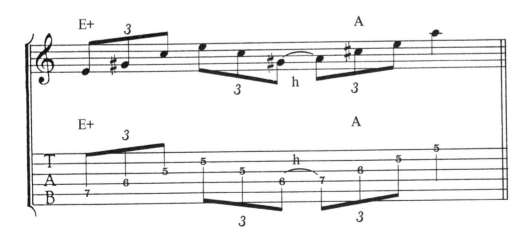

The II–V change is a very important one in jazz music, and often uses arpeggios to move through the chords. Here we see two examples, one resolving to a major chord, the other to a minor chord. Notice the slight change in the melody to accommodate the minor change.

182

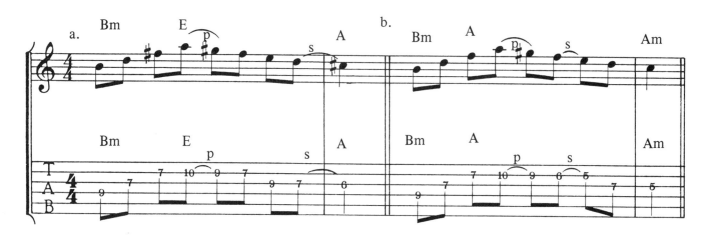

This arpeggio lick is heard so often that it has earned the label of the "minor cliche." It's still quite useful though, and I'm sure you'll recognize it as soon as you hear it!

JAZZ SCALE THEORY

The primary force behind most single-note jazz improvisation is the good old major scale. There are *four* different fingerings with which you should become well-acquainted, each one with its own unique texture and quality. Here are the four positions in the key of C. Pay close attention to the fingering in the tablature, and remember to stretch the *hand* to get to the notes, giving your fingers the proper workout.

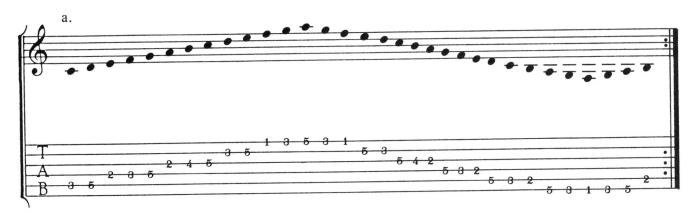

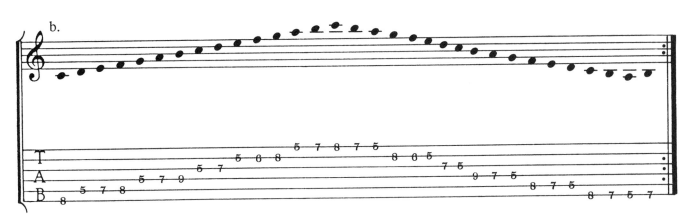

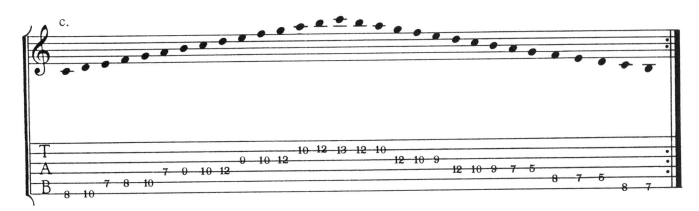

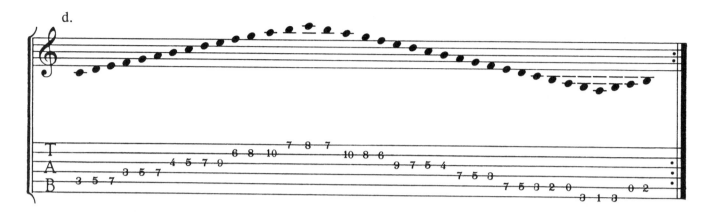

Improvisation

When using these or any other scales to improvise, they must reflect the type of chord over which you're playing. This is, of course, satisfying to you, but also communicates your special knowledge to the listener, creating a real "flow" of musical expression and ideas. Often in jazz, basic chord forms are substituted with more "exotic" versions such as sixths, ninths, major sevenths, and flat fives, necessitating similar changes within the single-note scales you're improvising upon. In the following example, we see how we can bring out the sixth more within our regular major scale to make some dramatic effects and changes. Take note of the positions on the fingerboard at which these sixths appear, and remember, if you want to be able to find them, they're always one whole-step, or two frets above the fifth of the scale or chord.

In this next piece, we're learning to bring out the *ninth,* or *second* of the scale. It's called a ninth to distinguish it from other seconds when it lies above the highest note of the scale's first octave. Note the new positions, and how similar they are to the sixths we were just working on. This improvisational exercise should also help train your ear to "hear" intervals such as sixths and ninths. These notes can be mistaken for one another at first, but the more you can recognize the notes of the original chords, the more you'll be able to hear these "new" notes as well. This is referred to as *relative pitch,* and is one of the more beneficial acquired skills one can get from learning music.

186

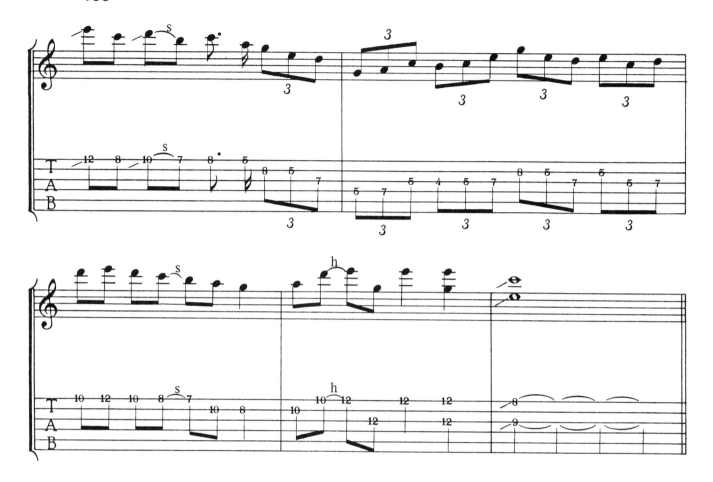

When bringing out the *major seventh* of a chord or scale, you must always be thinking a half-step *below* the root. This may seem to be a dissonance of the highest order, but can actually be an extremely pleasing change with which to improvise. Note how melodic many of the major seventh passages are.

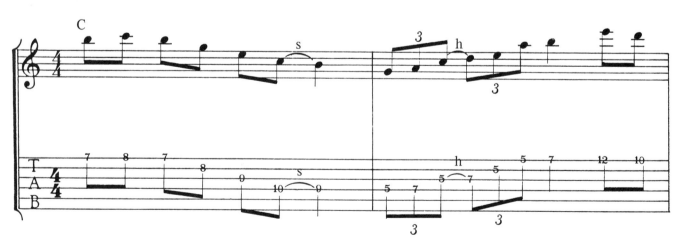

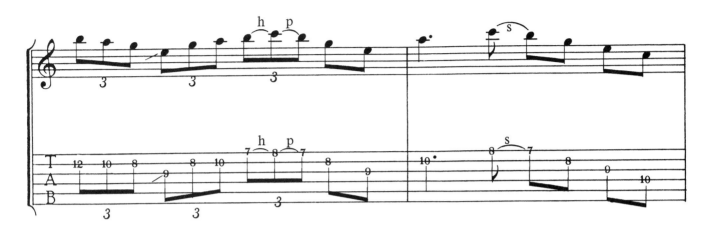

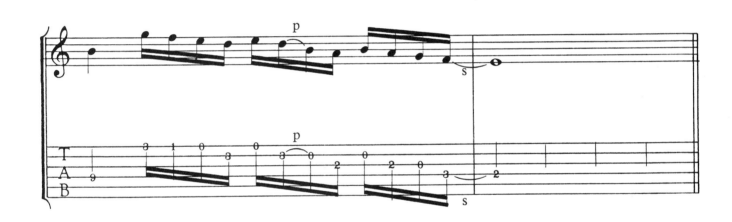

Full-Length Jazz Solo

This next piece, a full-length jazz solo, shows what you can do when you want to improvise around various changes using the sixth, ninth, major seventh, and minor seventh intervals. Because we are changing scale positions as well as chords, you'll now be seeing new positions of the intervals. Many will lie right beneath your fingertips, such as the major third of C (E), becoming the major seventh of F. If this throws you a bit, it's best to picture the chord form around the note to better acquaint yourself with just exactly where the note lies and what role it's playing. Be sure to always know just what chord changes and forms you're working around. Your ear will start to recognize the new notes after awhile.

188

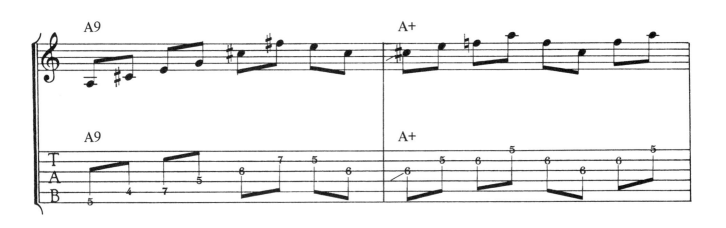

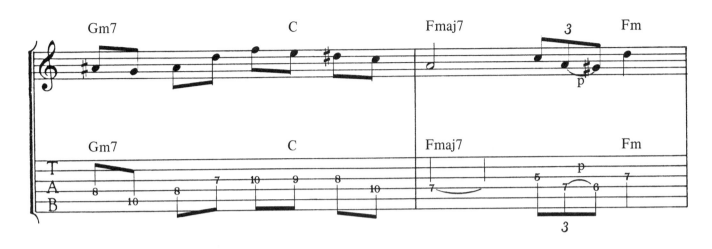

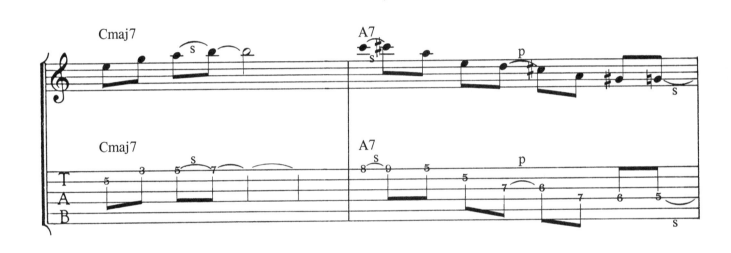

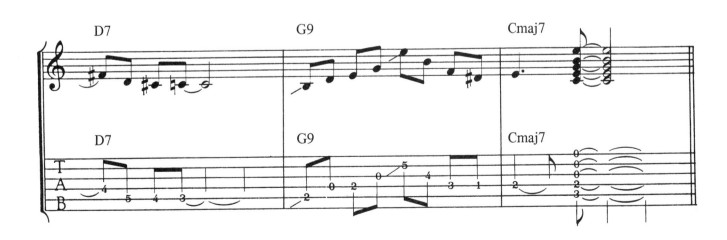

Learning the Various Modes

Ionian, Dorian, Phrygian, Lydian, Mixolidian, Aeolian, Locrian—these all sound quite intimidating to the aspiring guitarist, and with good reason. These ancient terms refer to the various "modes" of playing the diatonic scale, a concept not nearly as difficult as these names would have the modern player believe. They are merely seven ways of playing the scale, each one starting on one of the seven notes of the scale itself. For example, the Dorian scale of C would start on a D note, a whole step above the root C. These are the way the modes naturally sound playing in the key of C. Modes can be transposed to any key by preserving the key signature (and the relationship of whole and half steps).

Here are the various modal positions for the C major scale. Try to listen to the inherent differences between them, and try to determine which ones have a minor sound, and which have a major sound.

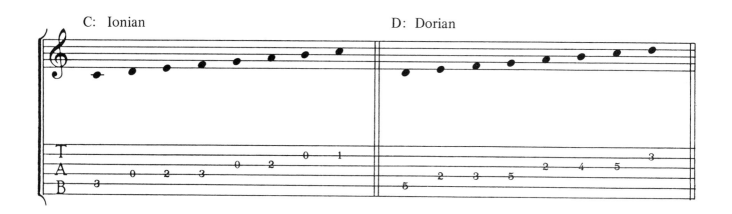

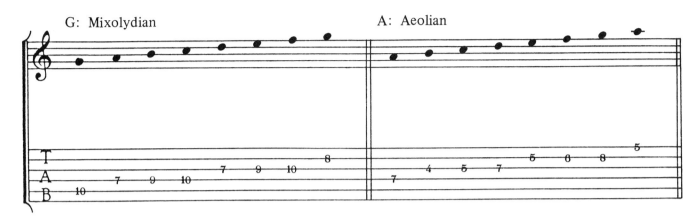

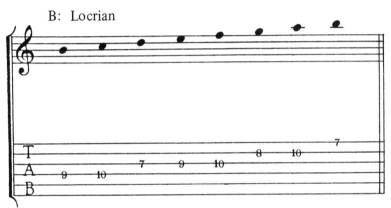

Now, we also see that the various modes also relate to different chords. For example, the Dorian scale that started on a D note within the C major scale, is now really a scale for D minor. Therefore, we gain a great deal of understanding about the origins of scales by using the major scale as a basis for all of the modes. You'll also find this to be an invaluable way of improvising, because you can now relate any given scale to its origin, and be able to find new positions all over the fingerboard.

This first piece shows some improvisational possibilities within the Dorian scale for D minor. Again remember, this is merely the C major scale, but we are bringing out and accenting different notes.

The E Phrygian is also a decidedly minor sounding scale, and therefore would only really apply to an E minor or as part of a blueslike passage, where dissonance is called for. Take note that the half step between E and F in this scale creates a rather eerie sound.

Em: Phrygian

The F Lydian scale has a very major sound to it, and relates quite strongly to the original C scale from which we derived these same notes. Also, due to the half step between E and F, we now see that this scale brings out the major seventh form of the F chord.

194

Fmaj7:Lydian

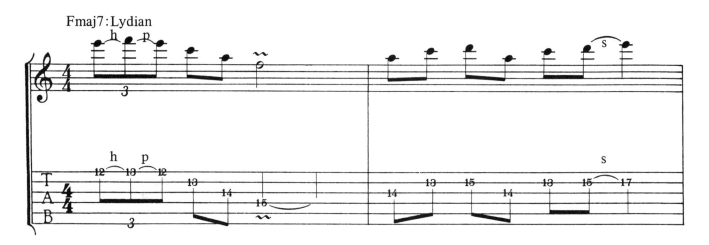

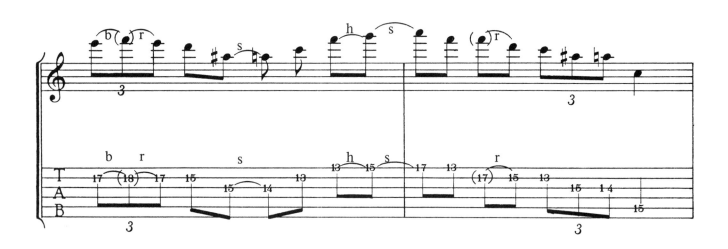

Now, as we go up to the next modal scale position, G Mixolydian, the F natural creates a *flatted* seventh sound, even though the scale contains B, the major third of G.

G: Mixolydian

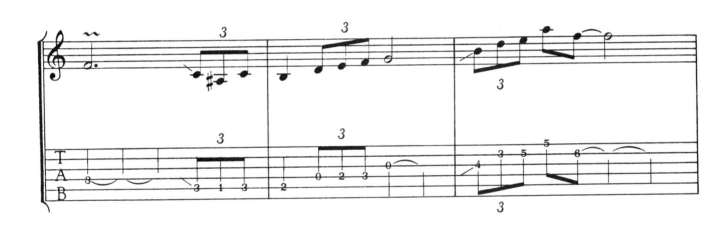

Finally, we see that the A Aeolian has a minor feeling, with the rather unusual addition of an F natural to the picture.

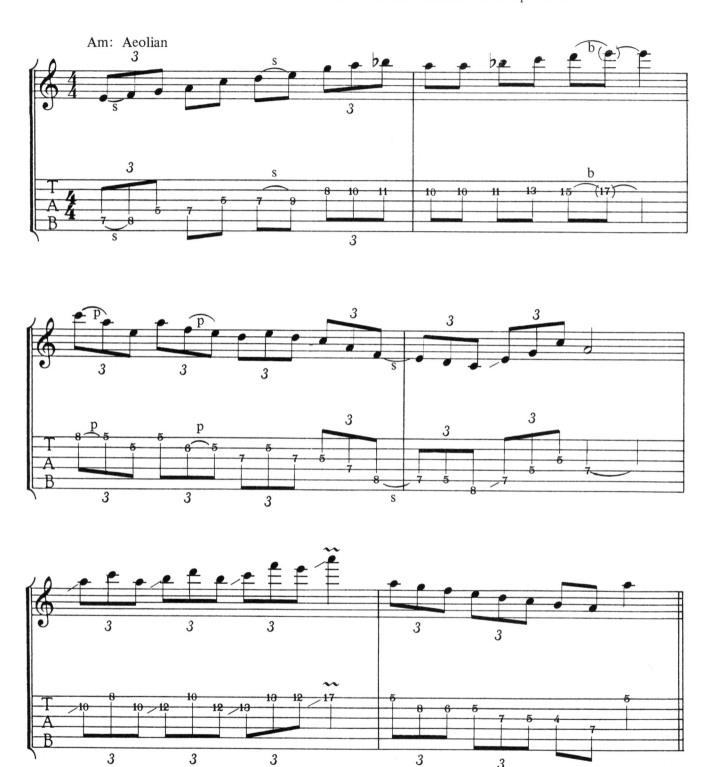

With the half steps both between B and C, and E and F, the B Locrian mode has perhaps the most unusual sound of all. These half steps create an almost "eastern" sound to the improvisations, reminiscent of what you might hear in the music of India or the Far East.

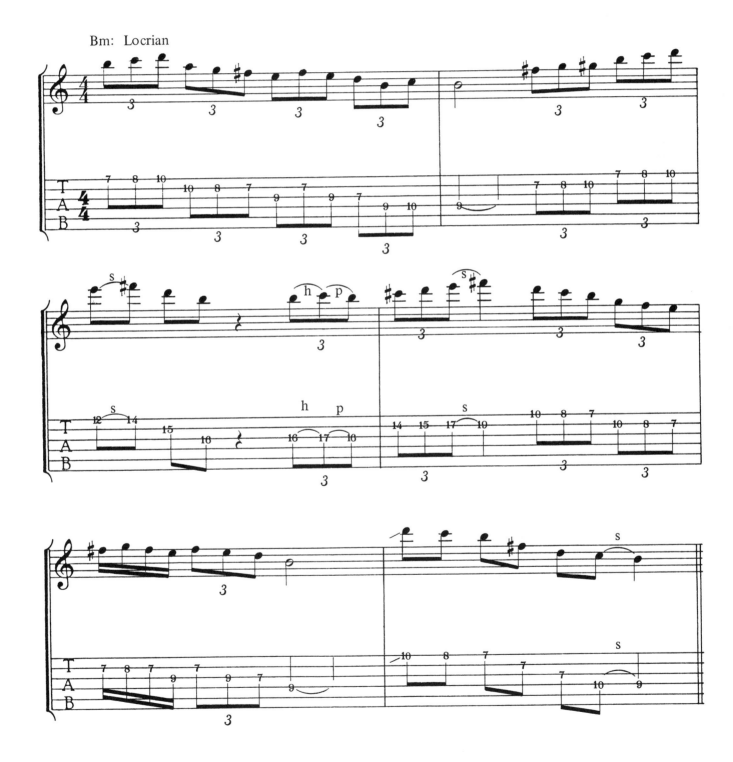

Practice these modes as much as you can, and after awhile, they'll really start to fall into place for you and your music. When playing them, you must be aware mainly of the notes you are trying to "bring out," or emphasize, that previously did not receive the same emphasis within the C major scale. This is the best way of coming to an understanding regarding the modes, and will certainly train your ears and fingers to create the most musical expression possible. Happy experimenting!

THE HARMONIC MINOR SCALE

No discussion of contemporary jazz styles would be complete without the harmonic minor scale. This is one of the more challenging scales with which to work, and offers much in the way of melodic possibilities. First, there are five basic fingering patterns to learn for the harmonic minor scale. Here they are for the key of C, both ascending and descending the fingerboard. Note that the main notes we want to emphasize are the minor third, the flatted sixth, and the major seventh. These notes combined create the unusual tonality of the harmonic minor scale, and in fact, the step-and-a-half jump between the flatted sixth and the sharp seventh is the most unique (and difficult to remember) facet of the scale. Because of these extreme jumps, it's necessary to get your hand used to the many *stretches* it must perform. Therefore, the "s" used in these exercises will stand for a "stretch" of the hand for positioning, rather than the previous usage for "slides" between notes.

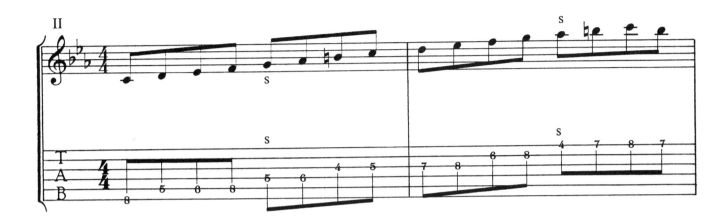

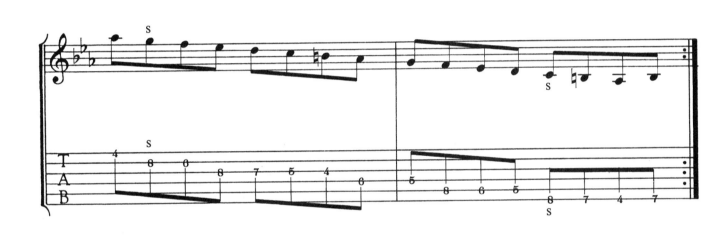

200

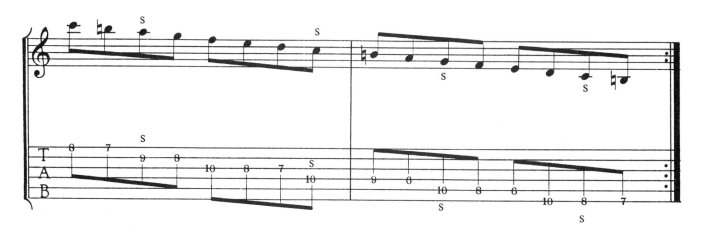

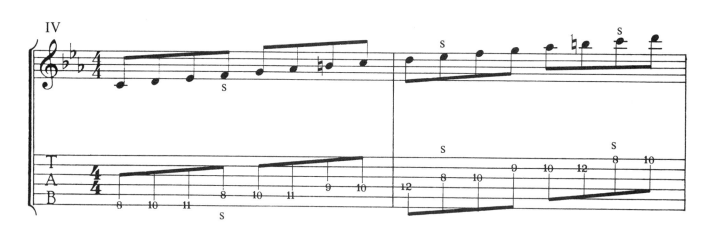

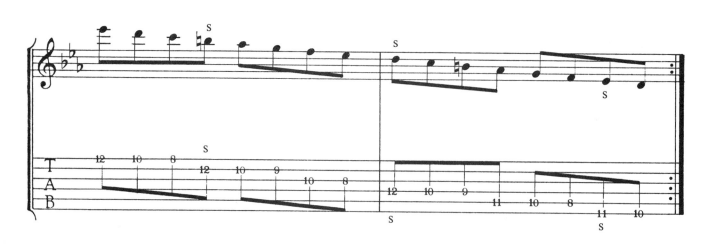

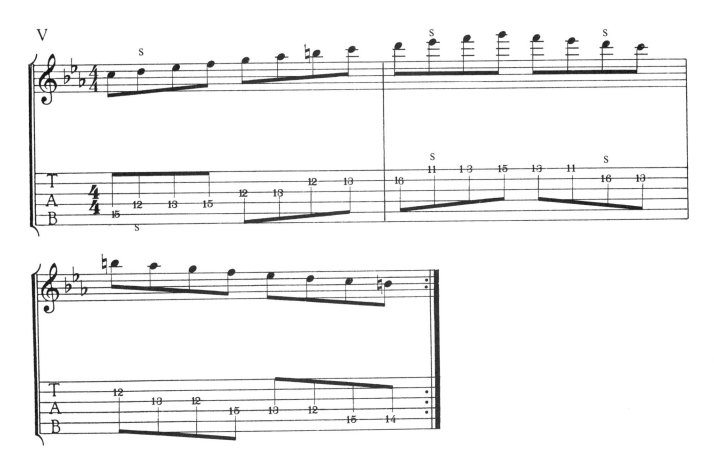

Now that you're relatively comfortable with the positions of the harmonic minor scale, I feel it would be a good time to experiment with it over some of the more commonly used chord progressions. These progressions are designed to bring the most out of the harmonic minor scale and its unusual tonalities. You'll note the use of many ♭5 and ♭9 chords due to these special notes within the scale. Keep in mind the many important stretches that are necessary to the proper execution of these various passages, particularly in the unusual minor sixth to major seventh jumps.

SOME NOTES ON PRACTICING

The concept of "practicing" your instrument has always been a somewhat abstract one to me, especially because I am a self-taught musician. It is, perhaps more due to the fact that I never once considered myself to be "practicing" because it was simply too much fun! Of course, this is the kind of spirit for which one should always strive, and is, I hope, what has led you through this book. Nevertheless, because I am your teacher for the time being, and I certainly have amassed years of experience with other students as well, there are some regimens I should be able to recommend.

First, you must be comfortable. By this I don't mean that you're lying back on your easy-boy chair, but rather that your guitar is easy for you to play, you sit or stand properly, and mostly that you feel good about yourself and your instrument. (This is true *even* if you want to play the blues!) I would recommend getting into the habit of playing at least 2 hours a day. Even if it is hard to find within your busy schedule, this time spent playing may become your most peaceful and meditative time of the day. Therefore, it's important to let your practicing become well-divided between disciplined exercises and more free-form improvisation. Because I am self-taught and proud of it, I always found my best way to practice was to create new challenges for myself, and to try to improvise with them to the best of my ability. I also found other players whose interests were similar in the sense that our jam sessions with each other would become challenging guitar "duels." This is healthy, because it establishes your ability to work with other musicians, and because hearing another musician's interpretation helps to give you new ideas.

Looking back, I realize that one very important aspect of my formative years was that even though I *was* always looking for new challenges and setting new goals, I learned to be basically content with whatever I knew at the time. This is important because each moment of a musician's development is crucial and must be assimilated fully. You may find yourself going through "stages," where certain forms of guitar playing strike your fancy and make your sound lean in a certain direction. This is fine also, because these influences are slowly shaping and molding your new, distinctive style. If you have a guitar hero, don't hesitate to want to "be" him or her for awhile. Learning the solos and styles of your favorite players is certainly advisable; just keep in mind that they did the same thing, while developing their own sound as well.

When playing the examples in this book, or any other for that matter, you must try to not overplay too soon. Try to play at an easy pace, allowing all of the notes to be properly enunciated. When you feel comfortable with the passage, you should then try to play it faster. I still spend some of my practice time playing my favorite runs as lightning fast as I possibly can, yet I know that warming up first will lead to less of a letdown when I do speed up!

Finally, it really is most important that you feel like you've accomplished something each time you've practiced. Try not to end on a discouraged note, although this helps some players to press on even harder during the next session. Enjoy your practice, be creative, and don't be satisfied until it sounds the way *you* want it to! Remember, it's *fun*, as well as *practice*.

7

ACOUSTIC GUITARS: WHAT GUITAR IS RIGHT FOR YOU?

This is a difficult question to address, and the decision depends greatly on your preferred style of playing. There are many variables to look for in an acoustic instrument—how it feels when you hold and play it; the width and thickness of the neck; and its type of sound, balance of tone, "projection," overall quality of workmanship, and appearance. This all may sound a bit alarming to the layperson, but don't be alarmed, for it really depends on how the instrument feels and plays to *you*, personally,

One of America's veteran acoustic guitars, The Gibson J-45. (Courtesy Gruhn Guitars)

and not to someone else. In other words, if you've developed your own style to a certain extent already, you should know the right guitar when you have it in your arms.

Perhaps the most famous jumbo acoustic of them all, the Martin D-28. (Courtesy Gruhn Guitars)

FLAT-TOPS

Over the years, the acoustic guitar has gone through a number of evolutionary changes into almost every size and shape imaginable. Some experiments were total failures, while others have remained the standard by which all acoustics are measured. Still, however, the experimenting goes on, and the luthiers of today continue to try to get the most out of the acoustic instrument. The acoustic guitar of days gone by was a small instrument by today's standards, and, prior to the introduction of steel strings, was of very delicate construction. The woods used in the construction of acoustic guitars do have a great effect on the sound, and this is a subject you should explore a bit before you choose your instrument. The majority of good acoustic guitars these days have spruce tops, with either rosewood or mahogany sides and backs. When buying a guitar with a spruce top, you should look for a tight, even grain with as few imperfections as possible. This not only relates to the sound, but to the top's ability to withstand climatic changes. This instrument, a custom-built Yamaha dreadnought (one of the largest and most popular shapes) has a sitka spruce top, with highly figured rosewood sides and back. This guitar possesses great volume and projection, as well as a nice balance of bass and treble response.

Yamaha L-53 Dreadnought prototype built by Terry Nakamoto.

The tone of most dreadnought guitars is usually characterized by a booming bass response, and although these guitars are relatively unbalanced in tone, they still remain very popular rhythm instruments. The dreadnought style first gained in popularity as part of the early bluegrass and country groups of the 1930s and 1940s. Seen in the hands of people like Jimmy Martin, Hank Williams, and other country greats, the demand for dreadnoughts soon overtook the popularity of the smaller guitars. Martin, the most important American acoustic guitar manufacturer, has always led the way in the construction of dreadnoughts. Its models have included the D-18, D-21, D-28, D-35, D-41, and the D-45. The "D" signifies the "dreadnought" size, and the numbers indicate an escalating degree of ornamentation of construction and materials. This esteemed lineup of vintage Martins shows the varying degrees of shapes and sizes of the 0, 00, and 000 lines, the next largest group of Martin guitars below the D size. Compare them to one another, and to the Yamaha dreadnought.

5 Martins: From left to right: 1908 0-18, 1926 00-21, 1888 0-28, 1931 00-40H, 1939 000-18.

Here is a close-up of the 00-40H's delicate marquetry and inlay work. All Martin models over number 40 feature varying degrees of mother-of-pearl abalone inlay work.

1931 Martin 00-40H.

Without a doubt, the rarest and most sought-after beauty of them all is the original Martin D-45. There were only 91 made from 1933 to 1942, the first being a custom-ordered model for Gene Autry. Most were made with a 14-fret neck-to-body joint, but there were a few, including Autry's model that were made with a twelfth-fret joint. Here is a very early 1936 14-fret model with a unique, extra-large body. This Martin D-45 was the fourth one ever built.

1936 Martin D-45, the king of the dreadnoughts. (Courtesy Gruhn Guitars)

Detail of the D-45's delicate, intricate inlay work. Note the "snowflake" patterns inlaid into the fingerboard. (Courtesy Gruhn Guitars)

In its very early days, Martin made even smaller instruments, in the size designations of 1, 2, and 5, with 5 being the tiniest. This is a 1937 5-17. Note its all mahogany construction, which makes for a very warm, even tone.

1937 Martin 5-18. Note its tiny scale. (Courtesy Gruhn Guitars)

Size 1 was a very popular early Martin style, and in fact, was quite a large guitar in its day. This is a 1917 model, and it features the beautiful "herringbone" marquetry so sought after and associated with all Martin models of the 28 variety.

1917 Martin 1-28. (Courtesy Gruhn Guitars)

As far as overall sound is concerned, I've found the smaller-bodied instruments such as the 0s and 00s have a more balanced tone and volume across all six strings. They are very well suited to fingerpicking because of this evenness of tone. However, if you're interested in lead playing and having the higher notes at your disposal, I would recommend using a model that joins the body at the fourteenth fret. Most modern acoustic guitars, with the exception of classical instruments, now join at the fourteenth fret, and in fact many manufacturers are offering acoustic guitars with *cutaways*. This is a major step toward helping the acoustic lead guitarists expand their range, and borrows one of the electric guitar's most attractive features.

One of the fine acoustic/electric cutaway guitars on the market today. The Guild F-45.

With regard to the woods used, I've noticed that rosewood tends to add more coloration and overtones to the sound, while mahogany and maple instruments posess a more even, straightforward tone. Over the years, I've come to prefer the latter for recording work, particularly when playing lead or fingerpicked parts. Martin, Guild, Gibson, Takamine, Yamaha, and Epiphone have also made several successful lower-priced models that use exclusively one wood for the top as well as the sides and back, usually mahogany. These come with my highest recommendations as fine guitars with balanced tones for beginning players who want something they can stay with for awhile.

ARCH-TOPS

Besides flat-top acoustics, which are certainly in vogue these days, the arch-top instrument enjoyed great popularity in the 1930s, 1940s, and 1950s. These guitars possessed an extremely even tone, and were first popularized through the big band era. Guitars weren't amplified yet, and the arch-top provided a very bright tone that worked well as a rhythm instrument that could cut through the sound of all the brass.

During this period, the name D'Angelico stood for the absolute pinnacle of arch-top lutherie, and these hand-carved beautiful instruments are highly prized collectors' items today. This is a photo of a very rare 1930s D'Angelico Excel model, with fancy New Yorker trim.

Early D'Angelico "Exel" model, with "New Yorker" trim.

Martin was one of the major manufacturers not usually associated with making arch-tops who tried to jump on the arch-top bandwagon during the big band era. Unfortunately, although their models were extremely well-made, they never really caught on enough to compete with Gibson or Epiphone. This guitar was their top of the line, the beautiful and rare F-9. In 1935, this guitar was Martin's highest priced model—$50 more than the fancy D-45.

1935 Martin F-9 carved top. Compare its neck and headstock with the D-45.

Most jazz guitarists today still use the arch-top variety of guitar, but usually in the electric, cutaway style. The days of the great acoustic carved-top instruments are surely gone, but thankfully those great Gibsons, Martins, D'Angelicos, Guilds, Epiphones, Strombergs, and Gretches are still finding their way to the hands of appreciators everywhere.

As far as your choice of instrument is concerned, it must remain a strictly personal decision. I've tried to help you by presenting some of the various types, with some tips on just why you might choose one over another, yet the final choice is up to you. Even when I go to the store with a student to help him or her find a guitar, only time will tell whether or not that particular instrument is really right for the style this person will develop. Be sure to go out and play a lot of them, because even the same models from the same year can be as different as night and day. Happy hunting!

ON THE ROAD AND IN THE STUDIO: ON BEING A PROFESSIONAL ACOUSTIC GUITARIST

In my desire to make this book as complete a coverage of acoustic guitar as I can, I feel it's necessary to spend some time sharing my thoughts, experiences, and advice with you. As of this writing, I've been a professional guitarist for 16 years. I must make the distinction in this chapter between acoustic and electric work, but of course, many of things I'll have to say apply no matter what kind of guitar you prefer.

My career as a professional began rather early compared to most guitarists, and this had both its advantages and disadvantages. Being catapulted into so many demanding situations while still young was a real test, and in many circles, you don't really get a second chance. As far as live work was concerned, it was, for the most part, a pleasure.

On the live stage I was allowed the freedom to hone my skills as a *communicator* of music, for I had to play, right there, for the people. Of course, being very young in those situations makes you a little more noticeable to everyone, and if you're good, they'll remember you forever as the "hot, *young* player." If you're bad, of course, they might write it off to inexperience, or you may simply be forgotten if you lack the aggressiveness to pursue success. Fortunately, I was one of the kids who was considered to be "hot," but I seemed to retain that "young and hot" reputation far too long, turning into a "seasoned veteran" overnight! These things are to be expected, though, as people become so used to pidgeon-holing anyone connected with music into a style, image, or what have you. If you are going into professional work at an early age, I can only say that you must beware of those older than you who will try to take advantage of your youth and drive for their own selfish benefits. I went through this, and while I was grateful to the many who gave me opportunities and recognized my skills, I now see how my sheer desire to be heard and my drive were, at times, manipulated by others. I can recall taking bus rides for hundreds of miles to play on albums that only paid my fare (if that). I know that far too many times I went into a live or recording situation without the wages being clearly spelled out beforehand. Needless to say, when this happened, I rarely made out as a wealthy kid! If you're offered a live or recording gig, make sure that you have a good idea what you should be getting paid for your work. Talk to some players you might know who've had these experiences, and get their advice. I can think of many times when someone like that might have helped me a great deal. As far as the whole live gig and touring question is concerned, my best advice is be careful not to be lured into a situation where you'll be underpaid with empty promises like "don't worry, you'll definitely play on the record," or "the next tour will pay better." These may in fact be true, and of course your judgment of character must play a part in your decision. But I know that I, even after years of experience, fell prey to lines such as these only for them to never come true. The problem is mainly that while an artist or manager who wants you to do a tour says he wants you to play on the record, the record invariably falls into the hands of a producer who, more often than not, has his usual group of players whom he feels most comfortable working with in the studio. This is a totally normal situation in the music business, and is to be expected. Try to take each gig for what it is worth in exposure and experience, and don't try to predict or expect what it will bring you later on.

Playing acoustic guitar, rather than electric, in a lot of those formative years enabled me to work on communicating in some very sensitive and delicate ways. I was touring with many folk artists, and I was often the only other person aside from the star of the show to take the stage. These were times of great musical development for me, because I was often learning as I played onstage. Sometimes, due to circumstances beyond our control, there would be no time to rehearse. But the artist, with great trust in my ear, would let me learn and perform it right in front of an audience. I would quietly sit there, listening, while he played a verse and chorus, learning the changes before I would jump into the arrangement. There was one performer whose chords were so predictable that I was right behind him, placing milliseconds between his playing and my learning. This was a very valuable time in my development as a professional player, and I would recommend developing your own ability to *listen,* and to recognize changes as a way of getting more and more familiar with the music you'll be encountering.

Studio work is, as a rule, quite a bit more disciplined than the majority of live gigs you'll come across. The reasons are quite obvious. Studio time is costly; therefore, you're expected to do the best work in the shortest amount of time. The studio environment can make you feel as if you're "under the microscope," with producers and other not-as-qualified personnel making all kinds of criticisms and suggestions, both constructive and useless. You must make every note count in the studio, for it's all being committed to the permanence of tape, and *that* is something that must stand the test of time. For the most part, a good producer is someone who knows how to get the most out of players with a minimum of stress put upon all concerned parties. This is not always the case, however, and you should be prepared for the worst whenever you show up at a session. Other musicians, particularly the successful, well-established kind, can sometimes misplace their energies in the form of improper attitudes toward the "newcomer" on a recording date or a tour. Just realize that they were once in your shoes, and for some reason, have some unresolved feelings that come out in the form of a cockiness directed at you. Pay it no heed, and just play the best guitar you possibly can. They'll soon be coming around to you, once they realize how important you are to the musical whole. Listen to what everyone else is playing—listen to the lyrics, the melody, and listen to the suggestions that are made. Listen, listen, listen, and your playing will reflect it! Also, don't get a head full of steam, as I have on many occasions, when you run across the type of producer who keeps saying things like "keep playing like "so and so" there!," or the classic "that solo was great, can you now do it again, exactly?" These can be very frustrating situations, and again you just have to chalk them up to experience. At times, using another guitarist's style as a guideline is really not such a bad way of communicating what is desired. It just sometimes feels like your own style is not getting enough of a fair shot. Don't worry. If you're good, it will come. It took years before I really started getting called for sessions where "my sound" was required, and that still doesn't make me immune to the kinds of producers I'm talking about, just a bit more tolerant!

The degree of discipline you must encounter can change as often as the weather. As a professional, you should always be prepared for this.

Having reached the pinnacle of acoustic and electric backup work with Simon and Garfunkel in summer 1983, I found myself under enormous pressure to play a very structured and non-improvised part, night after sweltering night. I was, however, lucky to be unleashed on a very few free solos each night, which seemed to make the other tension melt away. This is really what music is in a lot of ways, a build-up and release of tension. And as you can see, any given job can have a fair degree of both. It's all in how you handle it.

If you expect to be able to make it in the studios and on the road, you must have command of a fair amount of styles on the acoustic guitar. I'm sure there are players down in Nashville who are so typecast that they literally get called upon to play the same monotonous type of strummed part on every recording, even though they may be extremely well-rounded players. This is fine, and actually means security for a studio player because this person, in a sense, has created a demand for a specific thing he or she can do very well. And in the world of hit records, that's all that really matters. Eric Weissberg, the banjoist of "Dueling Banjos" fame, was long a mainstay in the New York studios on guitar, fiddle, and banjo, but when he "hit it big" with the *Deliverance* movie theme, he was flooded with work to play banjo on commercials for almost every product imaginable. The sound of the banjo suddenly could sell everything, and Eric had literally created the huge demand for *his* sound, single-handed! This is a rare example of an exceptional success, of course, but creating this kind of demand for "your sound" would be a great goal to shoot for in the course of your studio and live work.

As an acoustic guitarist, I'm often called upon to both flatpick and fingerpick on a session. Even on some of my own records, I'll play a fingerpicked rhythm part, and then overdub a flatpicked lead solo on top of it. If you've only mastered flatpicking, for example, there *are* ways around the fingerpicking dilemma, especially if you have a good ear. I know that Tommy Tedesco, the Los Angeles studio giant, *flatpicks* his classical guitar parts—something very unusual for this style of playing. Still, with his high degree of skill, he makes it work! Most of the time, if you're the only acoustic player on an all electric date, the parts you'll be required to play will be quite undemanding, and chord charts are probably all you'll have to read. The use of a *capo* will come in handy, because keys can suddenly change without warning in the studio, and you'll want to maintain the same positions and sound that you had before. For example, if I were feeling very comfortable playing a rhythm part in open G, I would use the capo at the first fret to maintain the exact same "feel," should the artist decide to raise the key to G♯.

This all reminds me of perhaps my funniest "musical mistake." In 1978, I had the good fortune to tour as guitarist for Art Garfunkel, a consumate performer, singer, and a true professional. This tour was sans Paul Simon, so whenever we played one of the old Simon and

Garfunkel favorites, I had to basically duplicate Paul's guitar parts. We had about 45 cities under our belts on this long tour, and had pretty much stuck to the same show, night after night. One fateful evening however, Art decided to take "Scarborough Fair" down a half step to E♭ minor from the usual E minor. He mentioned this briefly in the dressing room before the show, and all band members were present. We went out on stage, and the first hour or so went particularly well. Then it was time for "Scarborough Fair," one of the crowd's favorites, as well as mine. The song started with just my guitar and Art's vocal, and stayed that way, as in the Paul Simon version, for several verses before the other instruments joined in. The other players were a percussionist (on glockenspiel), whom Art had been giving a particularly hard time lately, and a classically trained cellist. Sure enough, after about three verses of just Art and myself, the percussionist entered by playing four of the most horribly dissonant notes you could imagine! The cellist soon followed suit, both of them diligently reading away at their own altered sheets of music, while Art glared at the percussionist with a look that could get you fired *10* times. All the time, John Jarvis, the piano player, who was out of this song, was frantically waving his arms in the air trying to get our attention before all the wrong notes took place. He had perfect pitch, and was able to hear that I, the faithful little guitarist, had *totally* forgotten Art's directions, and had kept the capo right at the seventh fret for E minor, rather than moving it down a fret for E♭ minor! The others weren't in the wrong; *I* was; yet the fact that I had played most of the song solo with Art made it seem like I was the only one in the right! Without a doubt, the longest "clam" I ever hit, the *entire song!* Needless to say, I 'fessed up after it was all over, and admitted that it was I who caused all of the problems, *not* the percussionist, whose job would've surely been on the line.

The author playing "Scarborough Fair" with Simon and Garfunkel, summer 1983. (Credit: Deborah Roth)

If you want to make it in the real world of music, you have to really believe in what you've got to offer. There are those who seem to possess limited talent, but are long on being able to sell themselves; while others are brilliant musicians, yet as insecure as can be. The latter is unfortunately the case in many a gifted individual. It seems that the sensitivity that creates the musical feeling goes hand in hand with the lack of belief in one's own abilities, and an oversensitization to others and what they might think of you. It's just one of those facts of life, and if you are one of these "sensitive artists," you'll just have to learn to live with it, and realize that you really are lucky and much-envied by those who wish they had your talent. Keep up the good work, and I know it will all pay off for you someday.

DISCOGRAPHY

To further aid in your development and appreciation of acoustic guitar playing, I have here provided a list of what I feel to be essential listening. All of the albums feature acoustic guitar playing, and are divided into the various musical categories.

Country Flatpicking

Doc Watson

   Home Again (Vanguard 79239)
   The Watson Family (Folkways 31021)
   Doc Watson (Vanguard 79152)

Clarence White

   Kentucky Colonels (United Artists 29514)

Country Fingerpicking

Merle Travis

   The Best of Merle Travis (Capitol 2662)
   The Merle Travis Guitar (Capitol 650)
   Strictly Guitar (Capitol)
   Walkin' The Strings (Capitol 1391)
   Travis! (Capitol 1664)

Sam McGee

   Mister Charlie's Blues (Yazoo 1024)
   Milk 'em In the Evening Blues (Folkways 31007)

Jerry Reed

   When You're Hot, You're Hot (RCA 4506)
   Me and Chet (with Chet Atkins) (RCA 4707)

Blues Fingerpicking

Robert Johnson

King of the Delta Blues Singers (CBS 62456) (CBS 30034)

Son House

Father of Folk Blues (CBS 9217)
Today! (Vanguard 9219)
Library of Congress Recordings (Xtra 1080)

Lonnie Johnson

Blue Guitar (EMI 7019)

Willie McTell

The Early Years (Yazoo 1005)

Blind Lemon Jefferson

The Immortal . . . Milestone 63738, Volume 2, (Milestone 2007)

Mississippi John Hurt

Mississippi John Hurt (Vanguard 19032)
The Immortal . . . (Vanguard 79248)
The Best of . . . (Vanguard 19/20)

Lightnin' Hopkins

The Roots Of . . . (Xtra 1127)
Early Recordings (Arhoolie 2007)

Ragtime

Blind Blake

Bootleg Rum Dum Blues (Biograph 12003)
Search Warrant Blues (Biograph 12023)

Bo Carter

Greatest Hits (Yazoo 1014)

Big Bill Broonzy

The Young Big Bill Broonzy (Yazoo 1011)
Do That Guitar Rag (Yazoo 1035)
Sings Folk Songs (Folkways 2328)

Slide Guitar

Robert Johnson (see blues fingerpicking)

Charley Patton

Founder of the Delta Blues (Yazoo 1020)

Blind Willie Johnson

Blind Willie Johnson (Folkways RBF 10)

Tampa Red

Bottleneck Guitar—1928-1937 (Yazoo 1039)

Collections

Guitar Wizards 1926-1935 (Yazoo 1016)
Mississippi Moaners 1927-1942 (Yazoo 1009)
Country Blues Bottleneck Guitar Classics (Yazoo 1026)
Steel Guitar Classics (Old Timey 113)
Bottleneck Guitar Trendsetters (Yazoo 1049)
Bluebird Blues (RCA 518)
The Voice of the Blues (Yazoo 1046)

Contemporary Acoustic Guitar

Many contemporary artists have utilized the acoustic guitar in
their arrangements. I would recommend the records of people
like: Simon and Garfunkel; James Taylor; The Beatles; Rolling
Stones; Don McLean; Dan Fogelberg; The Eagles; Crosby, Stills,
Nash, and Young; The Everly Brothers; Kenny Loggins; Glen
Campbell; John McLaughlin; Larry Coryell; Steve Morse; and Al
DiMeola.